THE SECRET MINISTRY OF JESUS

Pioneer Prophet of Interfaith Dialogue

William W. Mountcastle

D0905732

University Press of America,® Inc.
Lanham · Boulder · New York · Toronto · Plymouth, UK

Copyright © 2008 by
University Press of America,® Inc.
4501 Forbes Boulevard
Suite 200
Lanham, Maryland 20706
UPA Acquisitions Department (301) 459-3366

Estover Road
Plymouth PL6 7PY
United Kingdom

Library of Congress Control Number: 2007930031
ISBN-13: 978-0-7618-3833-3 (paperback : alk. paper)
ISBN-10: 0-7618-3833-3 (paperback : alk. paper)

The cover design is a stylized rendering of an ancient stone carving found in western China that features the Christian Cross emerging from the Buddhist Lotus, surrounded by clouds of Yin and centered on the brilliant Yang. This integration of Christian, Buddhist, and Taoist symbols dramatically expresses Jesus' ministry of interfaith dialogue and vision of world spirituality.

Table of Contents

Preface and Acknowledgements

Fascination concerning the amazing life and inspiring—sometimes puzzling and even shocking—teachings of Jesus of Nazareth, variously identified as Rabbi, Prophet, Messiah, Lord, and Christ, continues unabated from ancient days up to the present time. Recently, a flurry of discoveries of previously unknown scriptures have resulted in articles, seminars, books, and films that offer radical new interpretations of Jesus' life and teachings. Some of the faithful have been shocked into fury while others express their disbelief with laughter.

I have been motivated to write this book by some of the claims being offered but also as a result of years of teaching biblical and world religions. My dedication to trying to understand and follow The Way of Jesus was increasingly enhanced by insights from the other great religious traditions. My theology was changing, hopefully growing into larger visions of truth and spirituality. Specifically, the doctrines of the Incarnation and Atonement were morphing into radically different visions. Moreover, I was finding evidence that explained the connection of Jesus teachings with those in some Eastern religions. I was beginning to gain insights about the mysterious Mary Magdalene and questions about the composition of the so-called Gospel of John.

In the chapters that follow, I will attempt to develop these ideas more fully. No scholar should ever claim absolute certainty. The best we can do is claim reasonable assurance. The reader will find much relevant data that I believe is trustworthy, and I hope that my conclusions will be received as cogent.

In the matters of my personal faith that should be a part of any authentic theological work, I must say that my reconstruction of the Jesus story is not intended to be destructive of the heart of this great tradition. My hope is that it will help to liberate and exalt the true intentions and spirit of Jesus' life and teachings.

I reaffirm how important the years of teaching and learning from my students have been and continue to be. Several of my colleagues have also helped me to clarify and challenged me concerning some of my ideas. Dr. Lal Goel, Emeritus Professor of Political Science, read the entire manuscript and offered important suggestions regarding Sanskrit words and Hindu concepts. Emeritus Unitarian Universalist Minister Robert Eddy gave important and helpful suggestions in private discussions and also in the context of his insightful sermons. Dr. Pierre Kaufke, Emeritus Professor of French Language and Culture, shared with me the widely held traditions about Mary Magdalene in France. Ms. Jo Garber, Office Administrator of our Department of Philosophy and Religious Studies provided professional secretarial skills so necessary in this project. My thanks also to Mrs. Donna Fluharty, Patron Services Specialist, Curriculum Library, for assisting me with the cover presentation. After all the inspiration, teaching, thought crunching, writing and re-writing this book would not have come into being were it not for Mrs. Connie Works, Business Systems Specialist, who typed the entire manuscript—many times over! Her professional skill, patience, encouragement, and suggestions have been very helpful and much appreciated.

Chapter One
The Continuing Quest for the Truth About Jesus

The inspirations for writing this book came from several sources. First, as a long time student of world religions, I was led by current events and an increase in the number of Muslim students in my classes to gain a more comprehensive understanding of Islam. Because of my interest in the increasingly popular Jesus studies, I focused my inquiry on traditions about Jesus in the Qur'an. I had long been aware of the high regard in which Muslims hold Jesus, even though they reject the notion that Jesus was literally God incarnate and now a part of the Trinity. I remembered that in the Qur'an Jesus did not die on the cross nor was there an Easter event.[1] The questions that immediately arise are: What really happened to Jesus, and how will this effect Christian belief? These important questions will be addressed in this book.

The next challenge came from reading *Holy Blood, Holy Grail*, by Baigent, Leigh, and Lincoln. Here, the idea that Jesus escaped death by crucifixion is developed in great detail as a planned rescue operation.[2] This called to mind a book many of us had read back in the 1960s, *The Passover Plot*, by Hugh Schoenfield. An important difference is his conclusion that the rescue was unsuccessful, and Jesus expired. The Easter experience took the form of visions that came to his grieving followers.[3] One is reminded of Maurice Goguel's memorable words: "They did not believe because they saw him. They saw him because they believed". Schoenfield's interpretation has always bothered me because the world "plot" suggests a nefarious scheme whereby Jesus was trying to deceive people into believing that God had worked a miracle that was, in fact, a lie! This is quite unacceptable to me in the light of Jesus' extraordinary moral character and genuine spirituality. In fairness to Schoenfield, we should recognize that he did understand that Jesus enacted biblical prophecies to proclaim their meaning. If we substitute "drama" for "plot," we have a more acceptable theory.

It was this idea of a play that set me to thinking about the prophets of Israel who had inspired Jesus so greatly. I began to recall my seminary classes with Professors Elmer Leslie and Robert Pfeiffer and learning how the prophets acted out their messages in little dramas. It was not difficult to make the connection with Jesus' method of teaching that included dramas. Following that line of thinking, it occurred to me that Jesus' interpretation of the Suffering Servant poem of Isaiah could offer a perfectly reasonable explanation of why the crucifixion had to fail.

Even if he did not die by crucifixion the story is incomplete. What happened to Jesus? Where did he go? Again, one of Isaiah's Servant poems suggested an answer.

> And he said to me, "You are my servant,
>   Israel. . . .
> It is too light a thing that you should be my servant
>   to raise up the tribes of Jacob and to restore the survivors of
>   Israel:
> I will give you as a light to the nations
>   that my salvation may reach to the end of the earth."
>
> (Isaiah 49:3, 6)

Of course! Here was the answer. Jesus' ministry was unfinished. As God's loyal Son, Jesus had to carry the Gospel as far as his energy would permit. While I was pondering the question as to where he would go, I came across Joshua Benjamin's book, *The Mystery of Israel's Ten Lost Tribes and the Legend of Jesus in India*. This could be the answer to my question.

Another book came to mind. *The Lost Years of Jesus*, by Elizabeth Clare Prophet. On the basis of literature discovered in Tibet, she presents the idea that before his Palestinian ministry Jesus had spent his early years—from fourteen to twenty-nine–traveling through India and Tibet. Heretofore, I had not given much credence to this idea because I believed that Jesus did not need to travel to the East to learn about Eastern spirituality and ethics because Buddhist teachings had already come to Palestine. In the third century B.C.E., after converting to Buddhism, King Ashoka of India, sent missionaries to other lands, including Palestine. The Buddhist teachings of non-violence were accepted by John, an Essene, who taught them to his disciple, Jesus, so the theory goes. Maybe so, but Jesus could have discovered in his own tradition many prophetic teachings about non-violence.

Nonetheless, I was intrigued, did a very careful reading of Prophet's book, and was impressed to discover that she included bodies of quotations from ancient documents found in the Tibetan monastery library of Himis. They were stories about a Saint Issa whom the lama monks said was our Jesus. All of this could be dismissed as pure fiction except that the data was drawn from published books that included the testimonies of eminent scholars, very well qualified in the ancient Sanscrit and Pali languages in which the ancient documents were written and in the Tibetan language used in translating the texts to English. Moreover, comparative textual criticism was used to show the common themes about Saint Issa (Jesus) in the different translations made by several scholars at different times. But, Prophet's theory is about Jesus *before* his Palestinian ministry, and this does not answer our question about what Jesus might have done *after* the "crucifixion" unless . . . And concerning this, we will suggest a quite different setting for the ancient Asian texts.

The relationship of Jesus to Buddhism has long interested me. Buddhism had evolved from a non-theistic psychology to a theistic religion in the early part of the first century C.E., just about the same time the Jesus tradition was being developed. Could there have been a creative relationship there? This is another problem that we will explore.

Another source is *The Jesus Sutras*, by Martin Palmer. The title alone was enough to grab my attention. He offers a very carefully developed interpretation of an account of Jesus' gospel in Taoist-Buddhist terms recorded on ancient parchment scrolls and on a stone stele. True, this material was known to scholars years ago, but Palmer traveled to the site in northwestern China, discovered additional material and offered fresh translations. Was this more evidence that Jesus had carried on his ministry in the East—this time among the Taoists in China?

My purpose in writing this book is to give serious attention to these ancient traditions about Jesus, somehow, surviving death on the cross and then embarking on a second ministry in central Asia. I invite the reader to join me in making a serious study of the sources that I have identified to decide whether or not they are credible. The conclusions we reach will have a very serious impact on the faith we hold, whether it is Christian, Jewish, Moslem, Buddhist, Taoist, or Hindu. It may turn out that what has been traditional Christianity will have to be reformulated. It could be that these neglected tradition about Jesus' ministry in the East will offer us a new and exciting perspective on the gospel of Jesus and reveal the Son of Man to be a far greater person than has heretofore been appreciated.

We begin by turning our attention to the poet actors of ancient Israel—the great Hebrew prophets. Some may be surprised at the term poet actors, but it is perfectly appropriate as we shall see in the next chapter. Moreover, Jesus was grounded in the prophet tradition and also employed the technique of prophet theatre. This is the key that unlocks the mystery of Jesus' secret ministry.

Chapter Two
Prophet Street Theater in Ancient Israel

The Hebrew prophets burst upon the scene in ancient Israel about 750 B.C.E. with the ministry of Amos of Tekoa. Prior to his unique and revolutionary ministry, there had been first "seers" (I Samuel 9:9) and then "sons of the prophets" (Amos 7:14). The seers were charismatic holy men whose advice and disclosures about the future and lost items were often accompanied by the stirring music of harps, tambourines, flutes, and lyres (I Samuel 10:5). The "sons of prophets" (really precursors of the great prophets to come) were bands or "fraternities" of seers headed by the most effective member who was usually identified by name (II King 6:1).

Then in 750 B.C.E., the first of the true prophets of Israel emerged. He was Amos, by his own definition, a keeper of sheep and dresser of sycamore trees. Most important, he announced to Amaziah, priest of the sanctuary at Bethel, that he was not a seer "nor a prophet's son." (Amos 7:14). God had called him to preach judgment upon his own beloved Israel and Judah. He was the first true prophet and the first writing prophet who set the tone for the entire prophetic ministry that would culminate with the anonymous poet-prophet of the Exile in Babylon four hundred years later. What were the economic, political, and spiritual conditions in Israel during this period, and what was the content and nature of the prophetic proclamations?

The prophets lived during times of prosperity in Israel but they were also times when Israel was threatened by powerful neighbors and inward spiritual decay. Consequently, the prophets warned Israel to turn from fertility cult Baal worship, dishonest business practices, and foolish military schemes. It should be noted that the prophets were not primarily interested in predicting the future as is commonly and wrongly believed. They did not *predict* but rather they *proclaimed* as their Hebrew name *nabi* implies. It means speaker, literally mouth.

What did they proclaim? First of all, they warned Israel to change their immoral ways or face judgment from God, not by supernatural forces as is the case in the entirely different apocalyptic literature, but by natural and human means, e.g., drought, plagues of locusts, and military disasters. Secondly, they offered visions of an ideal future Israel based upon the Moral Law of Yahweh God.

Let us turn now and focus on the arresting style of their proclamations. First of all, they were all gifted poets who expressed themselves in the unique Hebrew poetic form of parallelism in which the second line develops or repeats the first. Instead of a rhyming of sound, we have a rhyming of thought. They expressed in very concrete images the most arresting, often shocking, ideas. Secondly, they were dramatists who often acted out their parables in the most attention getting ways. In fact, this prophetic theater may well be the most interesting feature of their ministry and, as we shall see, have the most incredible influence on world history. This should not surprise us, because these prophets believed that we humans, the sons and daughters of God, were to have, indeed, *must* have a part in making the prophets' oracles come true. In other words, all prophecy is self-fulfilling. God supplies the initial visions, the prophets proclaim them, and we then choose to follow or ignore them in the course of history.

Amos did not perform a drama in the sense of a play, but his great sermon in the temple of Bethel, in Israel, was certainly dramatic. Some would say it was the most dramatic sermon in the Hebrew Bible. He proclaimed that the surrounding kingdoms would all be judged for their ruthless military adventures by God's Moral Law. The revolutionary point is that there is only one Moral Law for *all* nations, and since the Moral Law is grounded in one power or author, there must be only one God. This powerful insight has gained for Amos, the title of the first ethical monotheist. All previous theology was only polytheism or henotheism. Moreover, Amos' congregation was shocked and offended to hear Amos pronounce judgment even on Israel for her sins of greed, false worship, and especially cruel, unjust treatment of the poor. Amos believed that God cares not for formal religion but that justice should become the ground of behavior for all of his children.

> I hate, I despise your festivals,
>   and I take no delight in your solemn assemblies
> Even though you offer me your burn offerings and grain offerings,
>   I will not accept them, . . .
> Take away from me the noise of your songs;
>   I will not listen to the melody of your harps.
> But let justice roll down like water,
>   and righteousness like an everflowing stream.
>
> (Amos, 5:21-24)

Hosea was a contemporary of Amos, but unlike Amos, he was a northerner and a tradesman. But his concern and message was compatible with that of his co-worker although his personal history and method of delivery were different, at least in one striking instance. Here, for the first time, we have a genuine prophetic drama acted out. Let us first note his great theme that perfectly combines with Amos' theme of justice. Hosea's religious encounter with God leaves him with the absolute certainty that God has told him: "For I desire steadfast love and not sacrifice, the knowledge of God rather than burnt offerings." (Hosea 6:6)

This is Hosea's love theme and when linked with Amos' justice theme produces ethical love. It is difficult to imagine a more perfect summary of biblical ethics.

Hosea's tragic domestic life provided the foil for his powerful insight that echoes Amos' insight that God cares not for formal religion. The way to worship God is to love Him in a deep and enduring way. The story of Hosea's broken marriage with Gomer was perceived by Hosea to be a parallel to Israel's broken relationship with husband Yahweh. To dramatize this, Hosea acted out the parable of his (and Israel's) broken relationships. Traditional interpretations are left at the sermonic level of Hosea's caricature of faithless Gomer as a whore who goes after many lovers compared to Israel whoring after the baals (the fertility gods of Palestine). But, Robert Pfeiffer suggested to his students years ago that Hosea chose to act out the drama by hiring a sanctuary woman from a Baal Temple (seen as a "whore" by the Yahweh people) and after a mock marriage, paraded through the streets to dramatize what a whore Israel had become to faithful Yahweh. He hoped that this drama, publicly acted out, would shock and shame Israel to repent and return to Yahweh.[1]

> The LORD said to me again, "Go love a woman who has a lover and is an adulteress, just as the LORD loves the people of Israel, though they turn to other gods and love raisin cakes." So I bought her for fifteen shackles of silver and a homer of barley and a measure of wine. And I said to her, "You must remain as mine for many days; you shall not play the whore. . . . For The Israelites shall remain many days without king or prince. . . . Afterward the Israelites shall return and seek the Lord their God."
>
> (Hosea 3:1-5)

Another kind of drama was enacted by Hosea, or we should say more accurately by his children. To emphasize Gomer's infidelity, he gave his children symbolic names. The first daughter was called "Not pitied" to show that God will no longer show pity to Israel. The next child, a son was named "Not my people" to illustrate God's alienation from Israel, and also, perhaps to express his own doubts about being the real father of his children. This was a terrible way to treat innocent children, we would say today, but Hosea was driven by a twofold despair: his wife's faithlessness to him and the faithlessness of Israel to God. To bring Israel to her senses, Hosea believed that the terrible truth must be acted out. His story concluded on a hopeful note. Most scholars believe that Hosea was reconciled and reunited with repentant Gomer as is recorded beautifully in the account of the second honeymoon:

> Therefore, behold, I will allure her, and bring her into the wilderness,
>   and speak tenderly to her. . . .
> And in that day, says the LORD, you will call me, "My husband";
>   and no longer will you call me, "My Baal." . . . .

> I will make you lie down in safety. And I will betroth you to me for-
> ever . . . and you shall know the LORD.
>
> (Hosea 2:14-20)

Notice how skillfully Hosea's words include both stories of reconciliation: Hosea and Gomer and God and Israel. Of course, this still remained only a hope but in Hosea's eyes it would be realized, perhaps because of his healed relationship with Gomer. In a sign of Hosea's faith in God's great gracious love, he changed the terrible names he had given his children to reflect the forgiving love of God. "And I will have pity on Not pitied and I will say to Not my people, "You are my people." . . . . (Hosea 2:23)

Isaiah employed the same kind of theatre when he visited King Ahaz to try to calm his fears about the threat of an invasion by Syria and Israel. As a sign that Yahweh would never allow Israel to be completely destroyed, he took with him his son, "A remnant shall return." In this situation, the name would seem to imply that there will always be a faithful number of Israelites who will return to follow God's way, and that will insure God's protection of Israel. In a similar vein, Isaiah named his second son "Spoil speeds, prey hastes" to help the worried king understand that Assyria is the new rising super power that will soon take out the threatening kingdoms.

Probably one of the most famous use of a child to proclaim a prophetic vision was when Isaiah referred to a pregnant woman, who may have been his own wife or Ahaz's queen, who would bear a child and during the time of his infancy, the threatening powers Ahaz fears, would be no more because they will have been destroyed by Assyria.

> Behold a young woman shall conceive and bear a son, and shall call
> his name Immanuel. . . . For before the child knows how to refuse the
> evil and choose the good, the land before whose two kings are in
> dread will be deserted.
>
> (Isaiah 7:14-16)

Of course, this is a messianic passage dear to all Christians. I do not have a problem with this quite different interpretation of Isaiah 7:14 because there is no good reason why spiritual insights cannot function from differing perspectives. Most scholars agree that Isaiah was dealing with a problem in his own day and had no notion of a Messiah seven hundred years in the future. And most certainly he was not speaking of a miraculous "virgin birth." But from a certain Christian perspective it is not difficult to see how this verse would come to be selected to support that doctrine, particularly when the Hebrew Bible was translated into the Greek Septuagint (LXX = 70 scholars), the Hebrew word *ha al-mah* (young woman) was, for some reason, translated as *parthenos* (virgin).

The most radical and certainly the most attention getting of all of Isaiah's playlets occurred during the period when Assyria was sweeping down on Palestine (711 B.C.E.) and Israel was looking to Egypt and Ethiopia for military support. In the tradition of all the great prophets, Isaiah vigorously rejected the military solution and predicted that Assyria would defeat both Egypt and Ethiopia and carry their people away into slavery. Nobody would listen to Isaiah until he took drastic measures to show what would happen to those who try to resist Assyria. They will be stripped naked. Like this, said the prophet, taking off all his clothes:

> At this time, the LORD had spoken to Isaiah . . . say, "Go and loose the sackcloth from your loins and take your sandals off your feet," and he had done so, walking naked and barefoot. Then the LORD said . . . "so shall the king of Assyria lead away the Egyptians as captives and the Ethiopians as exiles . . . naked and barefoot, with buttocks uncovered. . . ."
>
> (Isaiah 20:2-4)

This prophetic drama was not just a one-time performance either. The account explains that Isaiah walked naked and barefoot for three years as a sign and a portent! (v. 36)

The prophet Jeremiah next crossed the stage of prophecy, and he also dramatized his message. Some times the prophets would call attention to a drama not of their own doing but which they interpreted as a divine message. Such was the case when Jeremiah visited a potter's house and saw a pot "spoiled in the potter's hand" (Jeremiah 18:1-8). But instead of disposing of the ruined jar, the potter "reworked it into another vessel, as seemed good to him." The sensitive Jeremiah instantly saw this little drama as a way of understanding that Israel is like clay in God's hands, and there is hope for imperfect Israel, if she will repent and turn to following the path God has offered. To demonstrate what will happen if Israel refuses to mend her ways, Jeremiah acted out his own little playlet. He bought an earthen flask from the potter and gathering a crowd proclaimed:

> Thus says the LORD of hosts, the God of Israel, "I am going to bring such disaster upon this place that the ears of everyone who hears of it will tingle. Because the people have forsaken me. . . . Then you shall break the jug in the sight of those who go with you, and shall say to them. Thus says the LORD of hosts: So I will break this people and this city, as one breaks a potter's vessel, so that it can never be mended."
>
> (Jeremiah 19:36-11a)

Echoing the earlier prophets antiwar theme in his time, the uselessness of opposing Babylon's conquest of the Fertile Crescent, Jeremiah's costume became a wooden yoke to symbolize the Babylonian victory. He warned his astonished hearers that even though God has made the earth and is Lord of history, at this time, Babylon is destined to rule all and that, terrible as it seems, Israel must submit in order to survive (Jeremiah 27). The rival prophet Hananiah confronted

Jeremiah and broke the yoke proclaiming that God will not allow misfortune to come to Israel. Undaunted, Jeremiah returned wearing an iron yoke and proclaimed that Hananiah was a false prophet and, unfortunately, disaster will come to Israel (Jeremiah 28).

But the defeat and humiliation was to be only temporary and to dramatize his faith in God that a hopeful future is planned, Jeremiah bought a field in Anathoth in Benjamin, enemy-occupied territory, and made a public show of signing the deed of purchase. The message was that one day Israel would be liberated and Jeremiah would own land in free territory (Jeremiah 32:6-16).

But before liberation, there would be defeat by superior military force. Jeremiah believed that it would be pointless to resist and the most important thing was to keep God's people alive. In his most dramatic presentation, he mounted the walls of Jerusalem in the heat of battle and told the defending soldiers to surrender. "He who goes out to the Chaldeans shall live" (Jeremiah 38:2). His little play ended badly when the prince informed the king that Jeremiah's pacifism was treason. They arrested him and threw him into a cistern, "and Jeremiah sank into he mire" (Jeremiah 38:6).

Ezekiel was the next prophet dramatist. His ministry began at the end of the 6th century, B.C.E. while he was a captive of the Babylonians. The awesome mystical experience that came to him while he meditated by the Chebar canal was certainly great drama but it was not one that Ezekiel himself enacted. We only note that Ezekiel's vision of Yahweh riding in victory in his mighty war chariot through the swirling storm clouds left him with an absolute certainty of God's power and omnipresence that would, one day, deliver Israel.

But before deliverance, there came defeat for Israel and Judah, and Ezekiel acted out an elaborate drama to portray the tragedy. When he was still living in Jerusalem before conquest and exile, Ezekiel constructed an elaborate stage setting for his prophetic drama. Taking bricks and metal pieces, he built a model of Jerusalem with enemy siege walls around it complete with camps and battering rams. Then he acted out the attacks, lying first on his left side for Israel, then on his right side for Judah. He ate only the barest rations of food and water. He cut off his hair with a sharp knife and bound his legs with rope to symbolize captivity (Ezekiel 4 and 5). He proclaimed to his audience that this terrible misfortune had come upon Israel and Judah because they had turned their backs on their God who loved, and still loves, them.

> Thus says the LORD God: "Though I removed them far away among the nations, . . yet have I been a sanctuary to them for a little while in the countries where they have gone. . . . . I will gather you from the peoples . . . and I will give you the land of Israel."
>
> Ezekiel 11:16-17)

Scholars recognize that the book attributed to Isaiah is too long and too inclusive of history to be the work of one author. It covers hundreds of years of history with details that provide clues to the long period of time. That is why we recognize at least two authors; the original Isaiah of Jerusalem and an anonymous poet, prophet of the Babylonian exile (a disciple of the Isaiah school of theology?) whom we call Deutero or II Isaiah. He lived through much of the exile up to the time when Persia overthrew the Babylonian empire. Conquering King Cyrus had no need for the Hebrew captives and gave them liberty to return to their home in Palestine. This news was joyfully received and celebrated in Deutero Isaiah's beautiful poetry of return.

> Comfort, O comfort my people, says your God.
> Speak tenderly to Jerusalem and cry to her
>> that she has served her term,
>> that her penalty is paid, . . .
> A voice cries out:
>> "In the wilderness prepare the way of the LORD,
>> make straight in the desert a highway for our God. . . . "
>
> (Isaiah 40:1-3)

This provides us with background for understanding II Isaiah's theme of the Suffering Servant. There has been a great deal of theological debate concerning the identity of the Servant largely because of the great importance of the theme for Christians who identify him with Jesus. However, we will, for now, focus on what must have been Isaiah's Jewish view. In fact, in five of the Servant poems, he clearly calls the Servant, Israel (Isaiah 41:8; 44:1, 21; 45:4; 48:20; 49:3).

The Servant is the subject of these poems that celebrate Israel's release from Babylonian captivity so she may return to her Palestinian home. Here is a moving literary, virtual drama that explains Israel's captivity and suffering in terms of her failure to follow God's way as revealed by the prophets. Through suffering, she has learned her lesson and repented. Now she will be allowed to return to her ancient homeland following God's path to an ideal Zion of justice and peace. Moreover, the surrounding nations have been observing this morality play acted out on the stage of history, and hopefully, they too will repent of their evil ways and join Israel in building the ideal community. Here is Isaiah's great insight that the suffering of another, in this case the people of Israel, can be experienced vicariously and lead to choosing the higher path of living in accordance with God's ethical love.

> Surely he has borne our infirmities
>> and carried our diseases.
> Yet we accounted him stricken,
>> struck down by God, and afflicted.
> But he was wounded by our transgressions,
>> crushed for our iniquities;
> upon him was the punishment
>> that made us whole,
> and by his bruises we are healed.
>
> (Isaiah 53:4-8)

Did Isaiah attempt to act out this great drama? It would seem to be too great a theme to be presented by one person. But there is a hint in a section that appears to be autobiographical and reads very much like a part from the Suffering Servant drama.

> The Lord God has opened my ear,
>   and I was not rebellious,
>   I did not turn backward.
> I gave my back to those who struck me,
>   and my cheeks to those who pulled out the beard;
> I did not hide my face from insult and spitting.
>
> (Isaiah 50:5-6)

Very probably, Isaiah did preach that Israel deserved her prolonged suffering exile and needed to be purified. "Was it not the LORD, against whom we have sinned. . . ? See, I have refined you, but not like silver; I have tested you in the furnace of adversity." (Isaiah 48:10)

It is at least believable that Isaiah did act out, in part, the role of the Suffering Servant and was rewarded with a brutal response.

In this brief summary, we have documented our thesis that the Hebrew prophets were stirring poets who used a kind of street theatre to dramatize their messages. Their purpose was to keep the people of Israel focused on God's purpose for Israel—to work with God in creating a new world order of justice, love, and peace. We have set the stage for the next great prophet—Jesus of Nazareth.

Chapter Three
Rabbi Yeshua in Palestine with the Jews

Jesus, the heart of the Christian faith, has been given many titles: Rabbi, Messiah, Lord, Savior, and Christ. In the course of our study, we will discover several additional titles or roles that he bore but here we will introduce the title of prophet combined with rabbi—because although he was a teacher addressed as rabbi, his teaching and behavior were very much like that of the prophets. As we noted earlier, the vocation of the Hebrew prophets was twofold. In the first place, they warned their fellow countrymen to repent of their evil ways and return to following the way of God. The only predictions they made were short term, pragmatic ones that warned of the dire consequences if Israel did not change her ways. But they did not make long term predictions about the last things and End of the World as are found in apocalyptic literature. Secondly, in place of *prediction*, they *proclaimed* a vision of the components of God's ideal community of justice, peace, and loving fellowship. The centerpiece was ethical love toward one another twined with grateful and enduring love of God.

Quite clearly, Jesus fits perfectly with this prophetic pattern. Devotion to the Father god and ethical love toward one another are the two great Commandments, that are the basis of his ethos and the ground of Christian ethics. Although most of Rabbi Jesus' message was drawn from the themes of the Hebrew prophets that he so greatly admired, he did stamp them, indelibly, with his own unique personality. For example, one can discover by reading closely that Jesus interpreted Prophet Moses' Decalogue in a most radical way. He began by praying to God as Father, *Abba*, instead of *Elohim, Adonai,* or *Yahweh* that with the modifying title "Lord of Hosts" or "Commander in Chief of Israel's Army" carries too much militant baggage. Jesus' "modification of Torah" includes his striking non-vindictive teachings that develop the anti-war themes proclaimed by all of the prophets, except perhaps Joel who mistakenly calls us to "beat your plowshares into swords and your pruning hocks into spears" (Joel 3:10).

But the main idea that we wish to develop here is how Jesus followed the way of the prophets by using dramatic presentations of his great themes. Jesus, like the prophets before him, was an actor and a director. Moreover, he saw very clearly that prophetic visions do not become reality unless we make them to be so! Many mistakenly believe that prophecies are fulfilled by a transcendent God who magic-like reaches into the natural realm and by suspending the natural order, brings them to pass. Not so! We should realize by now that we do not live in that kind of a universe and that God is always right here working through the natural order as He/She designed it. Moreover, we should realize as Jesus did, even with a first century worldview, that God needs us, or at least has invited us, to be co-creators. That is, prophecies will only come to pass if we cooperate with God in making them happen. To stimulate our imagination, and will, Jesus employed the ancient technique of prophet theater.

I suggest that we can discover several of these dramas in Jesus' Palestinian Ministry. One seems to be a reflection of the first temptation as recorded in Matthew 4:1-4 and Luke 4:3-4. "If you are the Son of God, command the stones to become loaves of bread." It has been suggested that the temptation stories reflect Jesus' inner pondering as to what sort of a Messiah he would be. Of course, these temptation stories may be interpreted in various ways. Perhaps Jesus was tempted to use his special power to feed himself. But, I believe a more serious suggestion is the thought that the Messiah should feed all the hungry people in the world. We need not force a scientific world view on Jesus to conclude that Jesus' realistic understanding of life led him to see that only by learning to love one another will we begin to share our resources. Of course, everyone will have enough to eat when we care enough to share with our needy neighbors.

Then Jesus recalled Isaiah's wonderful promise about the coming of the Messianic Banquet. The Messiah will call all people to a great feast. Everyone will get all the food and drink they require, and it will all be free! The Messianic age will be a time of plenty. No one will go hungry anymore.

> Ho, everyone who thirsts,
>   come to the waters,
> and you that have no money,
>   come, buy and eat!
> Come buy wine and milk
>   without money and without price. . .
>   and delight yourselves in rich food.
>
> (Isaiah 55:1-2)

Jesus rejected this temptation because he saw that lack of physical food was not the whole problem. Spiritual food was needed to bring us to realize that sharing, not miracles, must precede eating. It was this insight, I suggest, that moved Jesus to begin his continuing drama of sharing table fellowship. Bruce Chilton explains that Jesus was teaching his guests that in the simple yet profound act of eating a simple meal in fellowship, we are making the kind of offering that God truly desires, instead of the bloody, smoking, mass barbeque priestly sacrifices that took place in the temple.[1] This is consistent with Hosea's proclamation: "For I desire steadfast love and not sacrifice the knowledge of God rather than burnt offerings." (Hosea 6:6)

Chilton believes that Jesus presided over these sharing, table fellowship meals throughout his ministry, breaking bread in his special way and beginning each meal with his own unique prayer to his—and our—Father God. I will suggest that these meals were really little dramas in the prophetic tradition. A promise—an appetizer, if you will—of the coming Kingdom of God, when everyone will have enough to eat because we have learned to share God's bounty with one another. This was Jesus' answer to the first temptation.

There is an interesting little detail in the Fourth Gospel (6:1-13) that supports our interpretation of these meals. It is the story of a boy who offers his five barley loaves and two fishes to Jesus to distribute among the five thousand people. Our modern worldview and understanding of Jesus does not allow us to believe that Jesus worked miracles that are contrary to God's natural laws. But, this story is certainly about a miraculous meal that satisfied a multitude with only a meager amount of food. What kind of a miracle was this?

We noted earlier that Jesus' purpose in these meal dramas was to invite everyone to have loving table fellowship with one another to promote the joy of sharing. We are told that Jesus had been teaching before the meal. Surely, sharing love was one of the topics. How refreshing that the small child got the message and offered all he had to Jesus. It has been suggested by many that this simple act started a chain reaction of sharing among the people who had not ventured so far from home without bringing some provisions. There are those who scoff at this idea of a sharing picnic, but I do not share their cynicism. I believe this interpretation fits well with Jesus' teachings and spirit and believe that this was, indeed, a miracle of sharing love. Moreover, this is much more impressive than a magic-like multiplying of food molecules.

Let us return to the temptation story and see if we can find a clue to another one of Jesus' dramas. The second temptation in Luke's account, it is the third in Mathew, seems to challenge Jesus to adopt the role of a militant-political Davidic Messiah who will use all necessary violence to bring in God's Kingdom. After all, Judas Maccabee had delivered Israel from Antiochus Epiphanes' hated rule with military force. The devil showed Jesus all the kingdoms of the world and promised them to Jesus if he would worship him. That is, Jesus must decide to use the methods of Satan—the ways of violence and corrupt government. Jesus answers: "Worship the Lord, your God and serve him only." (Luke 4:8)

Jesus knows full well that military violence is completely incompatible with the ideals of the Kingdom. He is in complete accord with the testimony of the prophets who had proclaimed that militarism is contrary to God's will. No matter that much of the pre-prophet material in the Hebrew Scriptures is filled with divinely ordained genocide, Jesus stands with his prophet predecessors who had completely rejected that barbaric tradition. His "Sermon on the Mount" provides us with several examples of his non-vindictive spirit.

One of the beatitudes proclaims, "Blessed are the peace makers, for they will be called the children of God" (Matthew 5:9). His revisions of Torah include: "You have heard that it was said, 'An eye for an eye, and a tooth for a tooth.' But I say to you, do not resist an evildoer. But, if anyone strikes you on the right cheek, turn the other also. . . ." (Matthew 5:38-39) "You have heard that it was said, 'You shall love your neighbor and hate your enemy.' But, I say to you, 'Love your enemies and pray for those who persecute you. . . .'" (Matthew 5:43-44) Luke's gospel used A Sermon on the Plain as background for Jesus' teachings and offers parallels in Luke 6:27-36.

Jesus goes beyond teaching us to refrain from using violence and offers us a non-violent way to resolve our differences. We can discover this neglected path if we realize that which we should have understood all along. Angry, hostile, and violent people are not healthy. They are, in fact, sick people. At the very heart of Jesus' Ministry was his concern to heal sick people and a careful reading discloses his formula for healing. If we agree that violence is caused by sick people in need of healing, we have only to employ Jesus' healing technique to discover his method of non-violent conflict resolution. To do this, we need to look at several of the healing stories that I suggest are an important part of Jesus' repertory of little dramas.

Let us begin with Mark's story of blind Bartimaeus. The first thing Jesus does is ask what Bartimaeus wants and the answer is "My teacher, let me see again" (Mark 10:46-51). If we will turn now to an account of two blind men, we hear Jesus asking a second question: "Do you believe that I am able to do this?" After they reply "yes," Jesus touches their eyes and says: "According to your faith let it be done to you." And, we are told their sight was restored (Matthew 9:27-31).

On another occasion, Jesus is not able to heal and Jesus is amazed at their lack of faith. There should be no question that we are hearing about faith healings in these stories and that healing depends on the faith of the supplicant. No faith, no healing. Today, we explain these healings in terms of psychosomatic medicine that recognizes the intimate connection of body and mind and the healing power of will or faith. Wonderful as they are, there is no need to introduce a supernatural explanation. This, of course, does not exclude God, rather it includes God's power in and through the natural processes.

If we use Jesus' healing technique as a process for resolving conflicts in a non-violent manner, we might translate from biblical to social language as follows: "What do you want?" becomes: What is wrong in this situation? Why have you behaved in such a violent manner? What problem needs to be addressed?" "Do you believe that I can do this?" becomes "do you believe that *we* can work this out? Are you *willing* to cooperate in seeking a non-violent solution?" "According to your faith, be healed," becomes "According to the degree that we really try to understand and cooperate with each other, we should be able to resolve this problem in a non-violent manner." Jesus' rejection of the use of force is one of the most important components of his Ministry. He has accepted the testimony of the prophets as to the futility of military solutions and, in his own experience under Roman occupation, he has observed the cruel treatment of God's children. Jesus' rejection of Satan's way in the temptation story offers us background understanding for the next drama that Jesus will direct and act out.

Jesus is well aware of the Zealot's underground terrorist organization and their plot to rise up and start the rebellion that will drive the hated Romans from his land. And, although he may have sympathized with their hurt and feelings of anger, he could not commit himself to join their ranks. Violence solves nothing; it only continues the cycle of hate. There are better ways to deal with our inhumanity toward each other. But the mood for vengeance and violent rebellion is very strong, and if Jesus is to be the one—Messiah or not—who leads God's suffering children into the Kingdom of justice, love, and peace, he must take a clear and dramatic stand against violence. He must make a public display of the non-violent path into the Kingdom. Jesus finds the theme he needs in the words of Zechariah.

> Rejoice greatly, O daughter Zion!
> Shout aloud, O daughter Jerusalem!
> Lo, your King comes to you;
>   triumphant and victorious is he,
> humble and riding on a donkey,
>   On a colt, the foal of a donkey.
> He will cut off the chariot from Ephraim
>   and the war horse from Jerusalem;
> and the battle bow shall be cut off,
>   and he shall command peace to the nations.
>
> (Zechariah 9:9-10)

Here was a prophecy of the Messiah that Jesus could fully accept. By non-violent means, he will destroy the weapons of war: chariots, war horses, and bows and bring peace to the nations. Jesus decided he would make a dramatic presentation of his true spirit and intentions and act out this ancient prophecy by riding into Jerusalem, not on a warhorse, but on a humble, non-threatening little donkey. All the synoptic gospels tell how Jesus prepared for the drama he was about to enact. On the Mount of Olives, just outside of Jerusalem, he instructed his disciples to go into the town where they would find a donkey. They are given permission to take the animal when they use the password previously arranged by Jesus. "Our Rabbi needs it." Jesus mounts the donkey and, with his disciples and a growing group of followers, rides toward Jerusalem. Some of them spread palm fronds in his path and begin to shout "Hosanna to the Son of David!" They have recognized that this is a messianic drama but they have completely missed the point of the donkey symbol. They cheer Jesus as a Davidic Messiah—a warrior king. Some Pharisees in the crowd are worried that the Zealots, or worse still, the Roman soldiers, might interpret this as the invitation to violent revolution. They tell Jesus to order his followers to stop this dangerous talk. But Jesus recognizes that he has failed to convey his message of a spiritual, not military Messiah.

Vincent Taylor correctly understands Jesus' response as a cry of despair, not of victory.[2] "I tell you if these were silent, the stones would shout out." That is: even the stones are infected with the false hope for a military, political Messiah. This interpretation is born out by the following passage: "When he looked at Jerusalem, he wept saying: 'If you, even you, had only recognized on this day the things that make for peace! But now they are hidden from your eyes.'" (Luke 19:42)

Jesus' little drama, so carefully prepared, ended in failure. He had invested so much time and energy into his teaching about non-violent conflict resolution, and he hoped that this simple drama would underscore it and be correctly understood. But the crowd then, as many now, looked for a military solution.

One more temptation story remains; number three in Matthew but the second one in Luke. I believe that the donkey drama can also be associated with this temptation because even though this temptation is about supernatural deliverance while the former was about military deliverance, they both include the need for violence whether human or divine. The Devil challenges Jesus to jump from the top of the temple to demonstrate his supernatural powers. He should not worry because God will send an angel to catch him just before he strikes the ground. Perhaps this vision came to Jesus while he was contemplating whether he should assume the role of the apocalyptic Messiah who was supposed to come diving in from outer space with an army of avenging angels.

New Testament scholars have long argued about Jesus' apocalyptic beliefs, and we need not cover this in any detail. Suffice to say, Albert Schweitzer represents the school that affirms Jesus' apocalyptic eschatology and C. F. Dodd asserts that Jesus taught a realized eschatology.[3] The former view stresses a future supernatural occurrence accompanied by dreadful violence. The latter view is of a non-violent, gradual, inward, spiritual coming of the Kingdom that begins with Jesus and continues to be realized. Luke's gospel summarizes it best. Once Jesus was asked by the Pharisees when the Kingdom of God was coming, and he answered, " The Kingdom of God is not coming with things that can be observed; nor will they say, 'Look here it is!' or 'There it is!' For, in fact, the Kingdom of God is among (or within) you." (Luke 17:20)

Schweitzer may have been correct in pointing out that Matthew, Chapter 10, makes a strong case for Jesus' apocalypticism because he sent his disciples out to proclaim the imminent arrival of the Kingdom and promises that even before they returned, the Son of Man will have already come, bringing the Kingdom. Of course, this did not happen, and this may have been the non-event that brought him to renounce the apocalyptic hope and his role as apocalyptic Messiah. But I believe that we can identify even more compelling reasons. Harold DeWolf, my professor of theology at Boston University, suggested what I believe are powerful arguments for concluding that Jesus could not, finally, subscribe to apocalypticism. Apocalypticists look for God to give up waiting for His wayward children to reform and, at last, imposes the Kingdom on us. This view is inconsistent with the idea of a loving parent-like God who patiently and hopefully works to elicit our freely turning to Him in loving obedience. Even more convincing, the Apocalyptic Hope includes much terrible violence as described in the "little apocalypses" and the Revelation of John, that is very clearly not consistent with the spirit and teachings of Jesus. Jesus' "growth teachings" about the Kingdom suggest a gradual and natural process that is much more consistent with the experience of the peasant, fishermen of Galilee.[4]

We turn our attention to another of Jesus' theology plays that is not suggested by the Temptation Story. In fact, the third play was a new idea for me. It is a play about resurrection that was suggest by the authors of *Holy Blood, Holy Grail*, Baigent, Leigh, and Lincoln.[5] The story begins with Jesus and his friends resting by the Jordan River. A messenger arrives with news that Jesus' friend Lazarus was ill. Jesus dismisses the matter with the words: "This illness does not lead to death; rather it is for God's glory. . . ." (John 11:1-6). Baigent and co-authors observe that it seems strange that Jesus waited two more days before returning to Bethany to tend to Lazarus. Then he tells his disciples: "Our friend Lazarus has fallen asleep, but I am going there to awaken him" (John 11:11). In the next breath, Jesus says he is "dead." When Jesus returns to Bethany, Lazarus has been in the tomb four days. His sisters, Martha and Mary are understandably greatly distressed, and Martha complains that if Jesus had only been with him Lazarus would not have died. Jesus comforts her with the words "Your brother will rise again" (John 11:23). Mary joins Jesus and Martha and with a group of mourners goes to the cave tomb that is covered with a stone. Jesus commands them to remove the stone and cries for Lazarus to come out. Immediately Lazarus does emerge from his tomb still wearing his funeral clothes, but very much alive.

The traditional belief is, of course, that this is another one of the great miracles that Jesus, Son of God, performs. In the case of John's theology, it is a "sign," *semeia*, not *dunata ergo*, or "mighty work" as in the synoptic gospels, that Jesus is the Messiah. Indeed, in John's interpretation, Jesus explains to Martha: "I am the resurrection and the life. Those who believe in me, even though they die will live. . . ." (John 11:26, 27)

Then, in what sounds like a minister's question and a congregational response Jesus asks: "Do you believe this?" Martha replies: "Yes, Lord, I believe. . . ." (John 11, 26-27) I had always thought that this account was another one of John's sign stories with little or no historical content. It was a confession of faith about accepting Jesus Christ as Lord of the Resurrection, but not to be understood as a literal physical resurrection of Lazarus. It is another one of John's "I AM" stories that ascribes divinity to Jesus.

However, the authors of *Holy Blood, Holy* Grail and the Jesus Seminar scholars, offer another explanation. In 1958, Professor Morton Smith of Columbia University discovered, at the Monastery of Mar Saba in the Judean desert, a missing fragment of the gospel of Mark that biblical scholars have named "The Secret Gospel of Mark."[6] Here is his account of the discovery. "Then one afternoon near the end of my stay, I found myself in my cell, staring incredulously at a text written in a tiny scrawl. . . . It began: 'From the letters of the most holy Clement . . . to Theodore . . . to praise (him) for having 'shut up' the Carpocratians." Smith concluded that this Clement, who identified himself as the author of *Stromateis*, was none other than the great Church Father clement of Alexandria. "The day after that . . . I came on an old binding . . . made by gluing together pieces of a fifteenth century manuscript. . . . I was able by soaking the pages to separate them and recover almost a dozen, several of which turned out to contain fragments of texts unknown to the standard editions."

Dr. Smith returned to Israel with the manuscripts to have them photographed so he could transcribe and translate them. The afore mentioned letter from Clement to Theodore reads as follows:

> You did well in silencing the unspeakable teachings of the Carpocratians. . . . For, even if they should say something true, one who loves the truth should not, even so, agree with them. For not all true [things] are the truth, nor should that truth which [merely] seems true according to human opinions be preferred to the true truth, that according to the faith.

> [As for] Mark, then, during Peter's stay in Rome, he wrote [an account of] the Lord's doings, not however, declaring all [of them], nor yet hinting at the secret [ones] but selecting those he thought most useful in increasing the faith of those who were being instructed. . . . Thus, in sum, he prearranged matters . . . and, dying, he left his composition to the church in Alexandria. . . .

> From this mixture is drawn off the teaching of the Carpocratians. . . . To them, as I said above, one must never give way, nor, . . should one concede that the secret Gospel is by Mark, but should even deny it on oath. For, "Not all true [things] are to be said to all men".

Clement now quotes the "false material" from the Secret Gospel of Mark.

> And they came to Bethany, and a certain woman, whose brother had died, was there. And, coming, she prostrated herself before Jesus and says to him, 'Son of David, have mercy on me.' But the disciples rebuked her. And Jesus, being angered, went off with her into the garden where the Tomb was, and straightway *a great cry was heard from the tomb* (Italics added). And going near, Jesus rolled away the stone from the door of the tomb. And straightway, going in where the youth was, he stretched forth his hand and raised him seizing his hand.

Clement concludes: "But the many other [things about] which you wrote seem to be and are falsifications. Now the true explanation and that which accords with the true philosophy. . . ."(Here the text broke off, in the middle of a page.)

Dr. Smith provides photographs of this manuscript in his book.[7] Dr. Smith next realized how closely the resurrection story in Secret Mark matched that in John's gospel and concluded that the resurrection of Lazarus was known to the synoptic tradition. He speculates further that John, anxious to dispel speculation about Lazarus being really dead, transferred Lazarus' cry from within the tomb to Jesus.

In concluding his account, Dr. Smith recalls that in the spring of 1963 he realized that secret Mark was not a reworking of Mark, but, indeed, was earlier than the canonical Gospel. In comparing John with Mark, he realized that the resurrection story in Secret Mark must have been the source both John and Mark had used.[8]

In Secret Mark, we learn of a woman from Bethany coming to Jesus and begging him to revive her brother who has died. Jesus goes to the tomb and hears a great cry. He rolls away the tombstone, enters, takes the man's hand, who is very much alive and raises him. The story continues that Jesus goes to the young man's home and teaches him about the Kingdom of God for several days. It also mentions that the young man is wearing a white linen garment. The reported cry that came from the tomb plainly tells us that the young man was not dead. Professor Smith believes that this was a ritual resurrection symbolizing death and rebirth just as is represented by the sacrament of baptism. Such Mystery Religion initiations were prevalent at that time, especially in the Essene community, who, asserts Smith, were identifiable by their white robes.[9]

As Smith has noted, the details of the story about the woman from Bethany being the sister of the young man make it very clear that this is a parallel of John's story of the resurrection of Lazarus. But, why was it deleted from the rest of Mark's gospel? Could it be that the detail about the cry from the tomb would make it impossible to believe that Jesus had really raised Lazarus from death? This would be a real threat to the developing Christ cult theology which is why Church Father Clement congratulated Theodore for quashing *Secret Mark*.[10] Secret Mark provides us with solid data for developing the belief that this was another one of Jesus' prearranged dramas.

The belief in the resurrection of the dead, either immediately following death as is suggested by Jesus alleged remark to the thief on the cross: ". . . today you will be with me in paradise" (Luke 23:43) or after "soul sleeping" until the Great Resurrection at the Last Day, was a central doctrine of Pharisee theology and hotly denied and disparaged by the conservative Sadducees. Jesus agreed in the main with the more liberal Pharisee theology and frequently referred to a life beyond the present one. It would be understandable that he would deem it proper, even necessary to include this teaching drama in his repertoire. Nor would this in any way disparage belief in the life to follow this present one. The purpose of the dramas would be to strengthen such belief. It would, of course, be perfectly clear that Jesus was giving, as he always did, full credit to God and not to his own ability to raise the dead to new life in the Kingdom. Of course, it is the latter that the Christ cult people would believe.

The next drama that Jesus chose to direct and act out is the powerful story of the Suffering Servant. We alluded to this earlier when we looked at the ministry of II Isaiah, who had come to understand Israel's suffering during the period of Exile as a time of punishment and purification. As the Lord's Servant, Israel had suffered for her own failure to faithfully follow God's way but, and this was Isaiah's great insight, Israel had suffered for all the other nations as well. They would, Isaiah hoped, suffer vicariously, and come to understand that they too must be faithful to God's will or suffer the same fate. As it turned out, this was not to be. The stories about Ezra's and Nehemiah's attempts at restoration are full of horrendous, cruel behavior to the Palestinians and the Jews who had remained in Palestine and intermarried with them.[11] II Isaiah's great dream that he believed was really God's plan for us was not realized. The cycle of violence resumed, and Israel was again plunged into misery. Now, here is Jesus living in another time of suffering for Israel; this time under the heel of the imperial Roman Empire.

It was during his retreat to the region of Tyre and Sidon that Jesus pondered the future of his ministry. Apocalyptic hopes had proven vain and a military solution to the terrible Roman occupation was too awful to contemplate. Even his teachings about ethical love and his striking faith healings had been misconstrued by his followers who concluded that he was either a military or apocalyptic messiah. So focused were they on a violent solution to Roman oppression that his drama of a peaceful, non-violent messiah entering Jerusalem on a little donkey failed to penetrate their understanding.

The great suffering of his people, Israel, drew him to ponder the thoughts of Isaiah and his vision of Israel's passage in the stream of history. Then, suddenly, it came to him: The Suffering Servant was not a future messiah but God's beloved people, Israel. Several poems make this perfectly clear with the phrase: "My Servant, Israel." The major theme of the Servant poems is that no matter what tragedy overwhelms Israel, God will never forsake His people. He will always provide for the rescue of Israel. Isaiah 53 makes this very clear. The poem is rich in details about the suffering of Servant Israel, "who poured out his soul to death." However, the Jewish Study Bible Commentary on the Tanakh clearly states that this phrase in Hebrew can mean up to the point of death but not necessarily dying.[12]

In order to clarify this point, we must take a closer look at Isaiah 53, focusing on the last part of the poem that describes the fate of the Servant. Israel has been "cut off from the land of the living. . . . They made his grave with the wicked and his tomb with the rich. . . ." (Isaiah 53:8b-9a) Isaiah is employing poetic imagery to describe Israel's defeat and captivity by Babylonia. But, after the work of vicarious suffering is done, and Isaiah hopes the surrounding nations have learned a painful lesson along with Israel, then *God will rescue Servant Israel.*

> When you make his life an
>   offering for sin,
> *He shall see his offspring and*
>   *shall prolong his days;*
> Through him the will of the LORD
>   shall prosper.
> *Out of his anguish he shall see*
>   *light.*

(Isaiah 53:10b-11a) (Italics added)

The main idea here is, that beyond the suffering *there will be rescue for Israel*. We may be very sure that this was also Jesus' understanding because he was very careful to twin Is. 53 with Psalm 22. We are all familiar with the heart-rendering cry of the suffering supplicant. "My God, My God, why have you forsaken me?" (Psalms 22:1a)

The poem continues with shocking details of his suffering. His hands and feet are pierced, he is scorned and mocked, and they cast lots for his clothes. But, we are not generally familiar with how the poem ends.

> From the horns of the wild oxen
> *you have rescued me.*
> *I will tell of your name to my*
> *brothers and sisters,*
> in the midst of the
> *congregation I will praise*
> *you. . . .*
> For he did not despise or abhor
> the affliction of the afflicted;
> *he did not hide his face from*
> *me,*
> *but heard when I cried to*
> *him.*

(Psalms 22:21b-24) (Italics added)

It should be obvious to us that Jesus understood Psalm 22 to be an exact parallel with the conclusion of Isaiah 53, and that is why he quoted the beginning of the passion psalm. Only his suffering and diminished strength prevented him from quoting the victorious conclusion. Clearly, Psalm 22 is not a cry of despair because Jesus felt separated from his Father. Not at all! He never felt abandoned. He used Psalm 22 as a proclamation of victory for himself, but more importantly, for his suffering people, Israel.

Jesus came to believe that God was guiding him to accept the role of Suffering Servant in another drama that would proclaim to his suffering and misunderstanding people that their God was the Lord of History, who would come to their rescue bringing the terrible Roman oppression to an end. But the drama would have to make it very clear that Israel would not be destroyed and that would mean that Jesus, acting the part of Israel, must escape death. Even so, the Servant would undergo great suffering and if it were to represent Roman persecution it might well be a Roman death sentence by crucifixion! Such a thought must have been frightening for Jesus. How could he survive this terrible experience? Jesus knew that some had indeed escaped death and there is literary evidence of this in the writings of Josephus.[13] His Essene friends were renowned as the leading practitioners of the healing arts. In fact, as we earlier discovered in the Secret Gospel of Mark, it was the Essenes who had instructed him in the symbolic act of resurrection that he himself had practiced, most dramatically for Lazarus.

All of this must have come together for Jesus during his time of solitude. Sacrificial love must be added to ethical love. But how could he share this powerful—and dangerous—plan with his disciples? On returning to Palestine and rejoining his disciples, he begins to teach them his new message.

> Then he began to teach them that the Son of Man must undergo great suffering, and be rejected by the elders, the chief priests, and the scribes, and be killed, and after three days rise again. He said all this quite openly.
>
> (Mark 8:31-32a)

The disciples are astonished. This must not happen to their beloved rabbi. Peter blurts out his objection and is greeted with Jesus' rough command to be silent! "Get behind me Satan! For you are not on the side of God, but of men!" (Mk 8:33) Sometimes even a gentle teacher must employ a shock treatment. Eventually his frightened and confused friends are brought to understanding and agreement. But now Jesus must develop the details of this heroic drama. Of course, he had done this before with earlier teaching dramas, but this one would present the greatest challenge to his creative skills and also to his ability to face extreme physical abuse. Jesus knew that only God's presence and powerful Spirit could guide him through this to a successful conclusion. Everything would depend on the conclusion. His friends must see him alive after the ordeal as a sign that God will rescue Israel from the tyranny of Rome.

Of course, we are assuming that Jesus planned and acted out this terrible drama. It took great faith and courage. Even so, no wonder his disciples in Gethsemane heard him pray, "Father . . . remove this cup from me" (Mark 14:36). Orthodox or conventional Christianity teaches that Jesus suffered and died on the cross as a blood sacrifice for the sins of humankind and a substitutionary death for each one of us. But, this is a late theological interpretation and not all Christians have believed this even from the very beginning of the story.[14] Some Christians find truth in Bultmann's question: "What has blood got to do with ethics?"[15] It is difficult to imagine a loving God condemning countless generations of His/Her children to damnation because of some "Original Sin" committed by the first human couple. Can any parent imagine offering his or her child as a blood sacrifice to pay for sins committed by others? We are told that this shows how extraordinary is God's love. Extraordinary, indeed! But I cannot accept it as resembling that which I know, or am willing to accept as love.

I suggest that Jesus had an entirely different understanding of God's will for bringing about a worldwide divine-human community of ethical love. Even though Jesus took it upon himself to play out the role of Suffering Servant, both the failed Israel of the past and the ideal Israel of the future that will include *all* of God's children, *it is absolutely necessary to play out Israel's victory in a final scene that shows that God rescues the Son of Man! Without the rescue, the suffering is meaningless.* Christians call this Easter and it is quite correct to identify this event with the birth of the Christian faith. The only difference is that most

Christians understand the "Resurrection" to be a supernatural act of God while we shall suggest that it was a natural act by Jesus' friends to communicate God's will for Israel. The fact that humans, led by Jesus' masterful role, played out this drama is no way diminishes the role played by God's Holy Spirit in the minds and hearts of the actors. It is another example of the truth of divine inspiration being proclaimed through human lives. In both interpretations, God is triumphant!

This powerful drama is so complex that it must be developed in a series of three acts. First, he must contrive to have himself fall into the hands of his enemies. Perhaps the confrontation would produce a last minute miracle and his enemies would be converted to be his followers. But, should all fail, he would continue to play out the drama. Until now, he had safely preached and acted out his gospel of radical love, without much success. What would it take to really get their attention and completely offend them? This answer came clearly. He must launch a frontal assault on the temple itself—the Holy of Holies. We noted earlier that his sharing fellowship meal dramas pointed out his disgust with the bloody animal slaughter and ghastly sacrifice presided over by the High Priest. Hosea had long ago proclaimed that God desired a relationship of ethical love, not animal sacrifices, and Jesus' open table fellowship meals were intended to dramatize that. Jesus determined to march right into the temple and challenge the greedy moneylenders and those who sold sacrificial animals for a healthy profit. He strides boldly into the Temple.

> And he entered the temple and began to drive out those who were selling and those who were buying in the temple, and he overturned the tables of the money changers and the seats of those who sold doves. . . .
>
> (Mark 11:15)

The account in John's gospel is even more dramatic:

> Making a whip of cords, he drove all of them out of the temple, both the sheep and the cattle. He also poured out the coins of the money-changers and overturned their tables. He told those who were selling the doves, "Take these things out of here! Stop making my Father's house a marketplace!"
>
> (John 2:15, 26)

In *Rabbi Jesus*, Bruce Chilton heightens the drama even more by suggesting that Jesus was not alone. He could not possible have overturned the heavy stone tables by himself. Over one hundred men, probably Zealots, were only too ready to assist Jesus in the token of violent confrontation. He even suggests that they were from the group of five thousand men that Jesus had met in the wilderness who were frustrated when told by their hero that he would never lead their military revolt.[16] This was Act One that was intended to precipitate his drama of the Suffering Servant.

Act Two of this drama would prepare his disciples for the terrifying climax. He feared it might be his last table fellowship with them. Appropriately enough, it would be the Passover Feast. During the meal, he would share with them the details of his plan. Of course, as was his custom, he must make careful preparations.

He arranged for a contact person to be waiting in town and tells his disciples to go into the city and look for a man carrying a jar of water. Anyone in the least familiar with middle eastern customs, ancient or modern, knows very well that only women carry water jars, very gracefully on their heads or shoulders. A man would not think of doing this and, in all probability, be unable to do so. Nevertheless, Jesus planned that his contact man would do this for the purpose of clear identification. He will then lead the disciples to the house for the celebration of the Passover meal and introduce them to the householder. Then they will ask Jesus' password question. "The Rabbi asks 'Where is my guest room where I may eat the Passover with my disciples?'" (Mark 14:14) The disciples followed instructions and all went as planned in preparation for the drama that would soon be played out.

But before we can move into the climax of this drama, indeed, in order that it will occur, a terrible deed must take place. Jesus had set the stage in the first act of this drama by directly challenging the religious authorities in the temple. That was the necessary condition, but there must now be a sufficient condition to trigger the arrest and trial of Jesus. His enemies need to know where and when to capture him without arousing his crowd of sympathizers and risking a riot that might bring the wrath of Roman soldiers down on them. One of his disciples must give the authorities the information they needed. Who was so loyal to Jesus that he would be willing to play the role of traitor and sacrifice his own reputation in the minds of those who did not understand the point of the drama?

Judas, freedom fighter, was courageous and disciplined and probably the most intelligent of the disciples.[17] He was the ideal choice to play the role of traitor and the two friends must have, together, developed the plan. This view is different from that of Schonfield who suggests in *The Passover Plot* that Judas was bitterly disappointed when Jesus refused to take direct military action to bring in the Kingdom by force. "Judas, therefore, betrayed Jesus, on this estimation, because he felt that Jesus had betrayed him."[18] But the words that Jesus speaks suggest that our view is more probably correct.

In the middle of the Passover meal, Jesus utters the shocking words, "One of you will betray me!" At least the gospel record tells us they were shocked. But, were they really? Yes, if Jesus' plans were secret, but he had been telling them about the suffering and dying of the Servant as it applied to him ever since returning from Tyre and Sidon. I remember my Boston University seminary professor, Edwin Booth saying, "Suppose the words Jesus spoke were 'One of you *must* betray me!'" and then, he adds, "It is the one to whom I will offer a morsel," and he gives it to Judas adding, "What you must do, do quickly." (John 13:21) Clearly, this is the signal that will propel the next part of the drama.

Jesus' open table meals expressed his conviction that loving fellowship was better than sacrifice but this last meal will go further. It will be the inauguration of God's New Covenant of universal inward spirituality that had been proclaimed by Jeremiah. Indeed, it sees to have been Jeremiah's main them.

> The days are surely coming, says the LORD, when I will make a new covenant with the house of Israel and the house of Judah. It will not be like the covenant that I made with their ancestors. . . . But this is the covenant that I will make with the house of Israel. . . . I will put my law within them, and I will write it on their hearts. . . . No longer shall they teach one another, or say to each other, "Know the LORD," for they shall all know me, from the least of them to the greatest. . . .
>
> (Jeremiah 31:31-34)

In the coming ideal world society, universal spirituality will be natural and instinctive. God's Will will be written in our hearts. The most natural thing for all will be to love God and love one another. This last meal assures the disciples that they will be included in the *Koinonia*, the new blessed community. But this time, the blessings over the bread and wine includes a somber note. The wonderful fellowship and ethical love that they have known with Jesus will henceforth include the sacrificial love that Jesus has come to believe he must dramatize for his contemporaries and, as it turns out, for all who hope for a world community of peace and love. Jesus had been pondering Isaiah's Suffering Servant message that, tragically, many of us will not be moved to repent and begin living lives of ethical love until we see the terrible consequences of our failure to live in harmony with God's moral law. When Jesus breaks the bread this time, in the persona of Suffering Servant, he will add: "This is my body broken for you."

But as we have discovered, the drama does not end with the Servants broken body. The victorious conclusion is that no matter how desperate the conditions, our loving God will never abandon us. His Kingdom of justice, love, and peace will become a reality and Israel's long history of suffering will be vindicated and capped with victory. Not a victory in another world or dimension, but right here on this world. Jesus always prayed: "May your Kingdom come, *on Earth*. . . ."

And now we come to the third and final act of Jesus' powerful drama. The idea that Jesus survived the crucifixion is not some radical new idea. Among the Gnostic documents in *The Nag Hammadi Library* discovered in Egypt in 1945, is "the Second Treatise of the Great Seth" that contains a description of Jesus surviving his crucifixion.

> And the plan which they devised about me. . . . I did not succumb to them as planned. . . . Those who were there punished me. (But) I did not die in reality but in appearance. . . . I was about to succumb to fear, and I suffered. . . . For my death which they think happened to them in their error and blindness; since they nailed their man unto

death. . . . It was another . . . who drank the gall and the vinegar; it
was not I. They struck me not with the reed; it was another, Simon,
who bore the cross on his shoulder. It was another upon whom they
placed the crown of thorns. But I was rejoicing in the height over all
the wealth . . . of, their error, of their empty glory. And I was laughing at their ignorance. And I subjected all their powers. For as I came
downward no one saw me. For I was altering my shape (appearance?). . . . For I passed them by quietly. . . . And I was speaking with
them. . . . And I was doing all these things because of my desire to
accomplish what I desired by the will of the Father above.[19]

Two features of this account are very disturbing. The idea that a substitute,
in this case Simon, suffered in place of Jesus is bad enough but that Jesus could
rejoice over the deception and laugh about it from a safe distance is completely
unacceptable. It does not fit the character of Jesus. The story of Simon carrying
Jesus' cross when he faints from the effects of all the suffering he has endured
appears in the canonical gospels. But, that incident does not mean that it was not
Jesus that was finally the one who was nailed to the cross and left to die.

The point of this drama that Jesus planned to act out was that Servant Israel
(Jesus) would suffer terribly before being rescued by God. The suffering and
agony was not to be faked. Jesus was the one nailed to the cross. The part about
Jesus laughing must also be put in proper perspective. Jesus hoped his people
would rejoice at the end of the drama because once again the Lord of History
has rescued Israel. This is the meaning of Jesus' laughter. Once again evil has
been foiled by the power of God. The psalmist expressed this in striking poetry.

Listen! The LORD in heaven is laughing! He holds the nations
    in derision.
                                                        (Psalms 2:4)

But the LORD laughs at the wicked for he sees that his day is
    coming.
                                                        (Psalms 37:13)

But thou, O LORD, doest laugh at them; thou dost hold all the
    nations in derision.
                                                        (Psalms 59:8)

God, the Lord of history, always has the last laugh.

Islam, the last great world religion, came into existence about thirteen hundred years ago and, as we noted earlier, its holy book, the Qur'an contains passages that plainly speak of Jesus' survival.

And for this saying: We have killed the Messiah, Jesus, son of Mary,
the messenger of Allah, they killed him not, nor did they cause his
death on the cross, but he was made to appear to them as such.
                                        (Ch. 4, *The Women*, Part VI, v. 157)

In his commentary on this verse, Maulana Muhammad Ali, a greatly respected Qur'anic scholar, summarizes the argument that supports this theory.

1. Jesus was removed from the cross after only a few hours but death by crucifixion took much longer. The two others on their crosses were still alive and to hasten their death, their legs were broken but Jesus was spared this because he was believed to be already dead.
2. Pilate found it hard to believe that Jesus was dead so soon.
3. The two criminals were roughly disposed of, but a wealthy disciple put Jesus in his own special tomb and cared for him.
4. When the women came to the tomb the stone had been removed, and that would not have been necessary in the case of a supernatural resurrection.
5. Mary saw Jesus disguised as a gardener that would not be needed by one resurrected.
6. Jesus, later, displays his wounds to his disciples and ate food with them.
7. When Jesus encounters two of his friends they do not recognize him. He apparently had disguised himself in his flight from Jerusalem to Galilee.

Muhammad Ali concludes: "Jesus did not die on the cross, nor was he killed as were the two thieves, but to the Jews he appeared as if he were dead.[20]

There have been several scenarios suggested as to how the rescue was accomplished. That outlined by Schonfield in *The Passover Plot* is, perhaps, the most carefully worked out.[21] Thirsting Jesus was offered a sponge soaked, not in vinegar, but some kind of soporific drug that caused Jesus to faint and appear to be dead. This would provide wealthy Joseph of Arimathia an excuse to ask Pilate for the body. To those who point out that Roman law would not permit a crucified criminal to be buried, it is said that Pilate was corrupt and would accept Joseph's bribe. Laurence Gardner, author of *Blood Line of the Holy Gail*, adds additional details.[22] Jesus was removed from the cross, unconscious but still alive and taken to Joseph of Arimathea's private garden tomb. There, Jesus was revived and his wounds treated by Essene friends who were reputed to be among the best medical practitioners. The fact that Essenes wore white robes would account for stories of one (Mark) and two (Luke) young men dressed in white at the tomb. In Matthew and John they become one and two angels.

Joshua Benjamin adds additional support to the rescue theory that is very similar to Schonfield's and Gardner's understanding. Pontius Pilate delivered Jesus' body to Joseph of Arimathea, a wealthy and secret follower of Jesus who placed Jesus' body in a cave where Nicodemus, a physician, used medicines to revive him. On Sunday, he appeared to Mary Magdalene as a gardener and then, secretly, to his disciples. Jesus tries to disabuse them of the false belief that he has been resurrected. "I am not a ghost. . . . Look at the wounds in my body. . . . I'm hungry!" (paraphrase of Luke 24:36-43)

In support of this theory, Benjamin refers to a leather parchment, discovered in Alexandria, bearing a letter from the leader of the Essene Brotherhood in Jerusalem to the Essene leader in Alexandria. This author asserts that he was an eyewitness to Jesus' rescue.

> I tell you only of the things I know, and I have seen it all with my own eyes and have taken a deep interest and an active part in all these events. And you know an Essene permits his lips to give only the strictest TRUTH.[23]

The letter continues noting that which we have already described. Some of the relevant quotations include: "The Centurion was friendly to me and ordered the soldiers not to break the bones of Jesus for he was dead." Benjamin paraphrasing the letter notes:

> Joseph and Nicadernus were seen binding over Jesus' face and they blew into him their own breath . . . (mouth-to-mouth respiration) . . . Jesus' face assumed a living appearance and his eyes opened . . . and he sat upright asking, "Where am I?"[24]

The letter goes on to explain how the Essene doctors continued to administer medicine to heal Jesus, kept his condition a secret, and helped him to visit his disciples. Joseph spoke to Jesus saying:

> "Knowest thou that the people who do not altogether understand your doctrine are meditating to proclaim you worldly king to overthrow the Romans? But you must not disturb the Kingdom of God through war and revolution. Therefore, choose the solitude, live with the Essene friends and be in safety that your doctrine may be proclaimed by your disciples" And Jesus consented that he would go into solitude.[25]

This letter from an alleged eyewitness of the crucifixion and rescue of Jesus is quite impressive and Benjamin believes that he has authenticated it in a footnote as follows:

> *The Crucifixion by an Eye-Witness* was first printed in 1873 and later again in 1907 by the Indo-American Book Co., Chicago, and was reprinted in 1977 by Syed Abdul Hayer in Lahore, Pakistan. It states that a member of the Abyssinian Mercantile Company discovered an old leather parchment written in Latin in an ancient house formerly occupied by Grecian friars. Archaeological discoveries indicated that the house was owned and occupied by Essenes.[26]

This would seem to be strong evidence in support of the rescue theory. However, we must note that the eminent New Testament scholar Edger J. Goodspeed expressed his doubts about the authenticity of this document. Some of these concerns are as follows:

Ancient manuscripts rolls are of papyrus, not parchment as claimed.

It is surprising that the letter was written in Latin before the middle of the first century.

The present whereabouts of the manuscript is not disclosed.

The author's acquaintance with the Four Gospels is difficult to explain since the author claims to have written only seven years after the Crucifixion and at least thirty years before the earliest gospel, Mark, was written.

The many Essenes are not named, including the writer himself.

In summary, Goodspeed writes: "The Crucifixion" is not the work of any eyewitness, as it professes to be, but of a nineteenth century rationalist."[27]

Goodspeed's observations reflect his keen attention to detail but I believe that there are good reasons for rejecting them because we can offer explanations that allow us to take seriously the claims made in the ancient letter. It is very probable that the letter has passed through many hands through the years and been copied in several languages on different kinds of material. This would also explain that the references to the four Gospels though unwritten in the early part of the first century were inserted later, perhaps to add authenticity. The puzzlement about the absence of Essene names can be explained by noting that the Essene society was very private and stressed secrecy. The fact that the present location of the manuscript is unknown should not come as a surprise since other ancient writings have been lost or hidden because they threatened orthodox belief as was the Secret Gospel of Mark.

I would also note that the details in the letter are perfectly consistent with the Qur'anic tradition and the Gnostic "Second Treatise of the Great Seth." All of this leads me to conclude that it is reasonable to conclude that the Essene letter should be included as evidence for the survival theory.

On the first day of the week, women, their number and names vary with each gospel account, go to the tomb to anoint Jesus' body but see the stone rolled away and the tomb empty.

> As they entered the tomb, they saw a young man dressed in a white robe, sitting on the right side; and they were alarmed. But he said to them, "Do not be alarmed; you are looking for Jesus of Nazareth, who was crucified. He has been raised; he is not here. Look, there is the place they laid him. But go, tell his disciples and Peter that he is going ahead of you to Galilee; then you will see him just as he told you.

> So they went out and fled from the tomb, for their terror and amazement had seized them; and they said nothing to any one, for they were afraid of. . . . (*efobunto gar*)

(Mark 16:5-8)

And, here ends the account of the earliest gospel. Mark's original story contains no details about the resurrection or appearance of Jesus to the disciples. Later editions of Mark contain a short and a longer ending that tell of Jesus appearing and giving instructions to his friends. What are we to make of this incomplete ending of Mark? What caused the women to be terrorized and amazed? Of what were they afraid? Scholars have long referred to this as the mystery of the lost ending of Mark, hoping one day, to discover it on an ancient parchment.

In the light of our theory, it really does not seem so strange or to be such a mystery. We can reasonably suggest that Mark belonged to the original group who followed the way of Jesus, that Mack calls the "Jesus People."[28] They understood the purpose of the drama and knew about it, and were thankful for Jesus' rescue from the cross and his resuscitation in the tomb. If the women who came to the tomb did not know about the details of the rescue mission they, of course, would have had good reason to be amazed and afraid. If, on the other hand, they did know, as I am assuming they did, they had a very good reason to be both amazed and afraid; amazed at the swiftness and perhaps even the success of the mission and even more afraid that the Romans would find out that they had been tricked and bring terrible vengeance on Jesus' followers. Using these ideas as background, let us attempt to reconstruct our own "lost ending."

". . . for they were afraid of what would happen to them if the Romans discovered the empty tomb and the plot to revive Jesus. The Romans would be furious as would Jesus' Jewish enemies be also."

The resulting turmoil could very well spark the Zealots to launch their revolution that Jesus had predicted would only bring total disaster, not liberation, to Israel. If Mark was writing after the terrible conflict had begun in 70 C.E., he might very well have added this comment: "and this certainly did contribute to the passions that ignited the conflict."

Of course, the "Christ cult" people, as so identified by Mack, would have their own motives for removing Mark's original ending. They could not tolerate an ending that was so completely at odds with the developing resurrection theology. As true believers in the Pauline tradition, they would have denounced the ending that we have suggested, and destroyed every copy of it that they could find. We know that this happened to other early Christian manuscripts such as the Secret Gospel of Mark and other Gnostic Gospels. Such is the misguided zeal of religious fanatics in all religions.

The very revealing and moving account in John's gospel tells of Mary weeping at the entrance of the tomb. Two "angels," (young men in Mark and Luke), ask her why she is crying, and she replies that she doesn't know where Jesus' body has been taken. She turns around and there is Jesus, very much alive, but he has been disguised to look like the gardener. But, when he speaks her name, she immediately recognizes him and rushes to embrace him but he asks that she not touch him, probably because his wounds are still painful.

Mary tries to tell the disciples that she has seen Jesus, but in the Gospel of Mary,[29] we are told that Peter will not believe her. He is admonished by Andrew who tells Peter that he has always been a hothead, and he reminds Peter that they all knew how much Jesus loved Mary. This, of course, is not at all unexpected if we accept the prevailing view of many modern scholars, that Jesus and Mary were husband and wife. Bishop Spong details this in his book, *Born of A Women*.[30]

Whatever the details were, the great drama had been successfully performed but now Jesus must make sure that the intended audience does not misunderstand. Of course, he does not want the Roman authorities or his Jewish enemies to know because their response would be only anger and scorn. Anger because Roman justice had been thwarted by a Jewish peasant and scorn because Jesus had feigned resurrection. Of course, Jesus had done nothing of the kind. He would never have done what God alone could do. But, he had acted out a role that was intended to dramatize what God would do for Israel—collectively and individually. His drama was intended to inspire hope in the hearts and minds of his despairing people just as apocalyptic literature is intended to do. In that sense, Jesus had salvaged what was good about apocalyptic eschatology that is otherwise saturated with blood and violence.

The final scene of this drama was absolutely critical. Jesus must be seen to be alive and well. His friends must not believe that he had been put to death. Then, they would surely loose faith, scatter, and that would be the end of Jesus' great dream of a new worldwide community of peace, justice, and love.

What I will now suggest is quite the opposite of what I and many others had previously believed. Formerly, to explain the Resurrection story, many of us suggested that the original appearances were visions that appeared to the grief stricken followers who would not give up their cherished memories of Jesus.[31] There are a number of these "spiritual encounters" where Jesus passes through locked doors, suddenly appears and disappears and finally rises into the air. But, there are also parallel stories in which Jesus displays his wounds, asks for food and eats, invites his friends to touch him and feel his skin and bones. He even declares, as we noted above, that he is not a ghost! (Luke 24:36-43) He also says that he is hungry (Luke 24:41). Paul preached that the resurrected boy will be a *spiritual body* but the words of Jesus clearly refers to a normal physical body. Many of us had heretofore believed that these stories of physical resurrection were later creations intended to strengthen the Resurrection faith. But, I have come to believe just the opposite. The physical stories came first because Jesus wanted to make very sure that his disciples and friends knew that there was no deception about the drama he had performed. He wanted his followers to know that just as he had been rescued, so will Israel be delivered from her present suffering under the Romans as Isaiah had proclaimed. He had never intended that they believe that he had been raised from the dead. That idea was a creation of Paul and the gentile Christ cult people. They had not known the historical Jesus and only wanted to use Jesus' charismatic spirit and healing ability to buttress the ancient fertility religion of a dying raising deity. But, Jesus had no part in developing that mistaken theology. He told his own wonderful story, that involved neither deception nor the resurrection of his corpse.

Of course, once Jesus' drama had been successfully played out, his Palestinian ministry was finished. He had taught his disciples about the Kingdom of his Father, using the great themes of the Hebrew prophets that preceded him. Instead of a detailed system of ethics, he had taught by living his non-violent ethos and ministry of caring and healing. Most important and striking was his own unique lived out presentation of the divine nature. His disciples were overpowered by his charismatic personality and came to confess that to be in the presence of Jesus was to be in God's presence as well. It was Jesus' powerful baptism experience of God's intimate presence and acceptance of him as a son that inspired and sustained his entire ministry.[32] The very idea that anyone could deny the existence of his loving God was absolutely beyond his comprehension. It is this passionate belief that provides us with a clue for the next drama in his ministry.

At the very beginning of his spiritual life in early years at home, he had studied the prophetic teachings and learned of their rejection of violence and war. Many scholars believe that Jesus spent time with John, perhaps in Qumran, learning about Essene beliefs that included non-violence. We suggested earlier that these ideas that would reinforce the prophetic ethics, may have been brought to Palestine by Buddhist missionaries sent by converted Indian King Ashoka in the third century B.C.E.[33] These early Theravada Buddhists were non-theists because Sidhartha Gautama Buddha had avoided metaphysical speculation and dedicated his entire ministry to teaching his followers the causes of suffering and how to overcome it.

Jesus must have greatly admired Buddha's teachings about non-violence and compassion for all living beings and the meditative techniques that could abolish suffering but he must have found it impossible to understand how any sensitive person could be unaware of God's presence. Jesus wanted to learn more about the compassionate Buddhists but he also felt driven to share with them his own experience of the loving father God who was his constant Companion. This is one clue to answering the question: Where did Jesus go and what was the content of his ministry after leaving Palestine? We find support for this idea of a post Palestinian ministry in Asia in another Servant poem.

> And he said to me, "You are my servant,
>   Israel. . . ."
> "It is too light a thing that you should be my servant
>   to raise up the tribes of Jacob
>   and to restore the survivors of Israel:
> I will give you as a light to the nations,
>   that my salvation may reach to the end of the earth."
>
>   (Isaiah 49:3,6)

It was this Servant Poem that next gripped Jesus' imagination. His Ministry was not over. There remained one more drama to be played out. It would be the drama of Servant Israel as Missionary to the World.

Chapter Four
Saint Issa in India with the Hindus

But, where did Jesus go after his rescue from the Cross and the tomb? Some ancient Indian and Moslem legends claim that he traveled east to India and Kashmir.[1] Other traditions tell of Jesus in Tibet and perhaps even in China. In any event, it would have been dangerous for Jesus to have remained in Palestine. He would surely have been recognized, sooner or later, and that would have been fatal for him and, also, threatening for his family and friends who had arranged the rescue mission and deceived the Romans. The most compelling evidence tell us that Jesus first traveled to India.

Why did he choose India instead of closer Egypt or Syria? We have suggested that Jesus may have learned from the Essenes of the Buddhist roots that supported his teachings and after his ministry in Palestine and his harrowing escape, he was moved by a desire to visit the Buddhists on their home ground where he could learn more of their teachings that were so congenial to his own.[2] But more important, was his burning desire to share with the non-theistic Buddhists of the "ancient school" that we call Theravada, his own life changing religious experience during his baptism when he experienced a direct mystical encounter with the Holy One he came to call Abba or Father. I believe that Jesus realized that Buddhist compassion is groundless without his Father-God, who grounds all compassion. In other words, Jesus decided to journey to India as the Missionary Servant Israel, teaching about the loving Father God and his vision of a wonderful all embracing community of justice, peace, and love—the Kingdom of God. This was to be missionary work in the best sense; not conversion but sharing. Jesus would carry his gift to those who had gifted him. Of course, this theory reverses the previously mentioned theory that Jesus had lived in the East prior to his ministry. We are suggesting that Jesus traveled to India *after* his ministry in Palestine.

The theory that Jesus traveled to India has been developed most recently by Joshua M. Benjamin in his book *The Mystery of Israel's Ten Lost Tribes and the Legend of Jesus in India*. He believes that the strongest evidence is found in the Syrian version of *The Acts of Judas Thomas* even though it is labeled "apocryphal" or of uncertain authorship. He argues that the term apocryphal really means hidden and applied to those writings that were considered so very important that they must be hidden from all except the inner circle of believers. In defense of the historical verity of the story, Benjamin notes that the King Gondahorus in one of the adventures was a historical person as is verified by coins bearing his name. The King's name is sometimes spelled Gudnaphar or Gundephar. Benjamin believes that despite minor variations in spelling all three names refer to the same historical person.[3]

Syrian Acts contains explicit language that Thomas was accompanied by Jesus on the missionary journey to India. Benjamin provides us with the salient points of this tradition. However before we do this, I would like to share with the reader some critical observations about this Syriac text that is both fascinating and controversial. I obtained a copy of it in the Semitic Study Series, New Series, Edited by J. H. Hoopers and T. Jansma, and published in 1952. Jansma's critical comments are based on the translation and comments of F. C. Burkitt, first published by Cambridge University Press in 1899 and more recently by Gorgias Press in 2002.

Burkitt offers his reasons for regarding the authenticity and critical importance of this document. He first points out that Christianity was not at first a Greek religion despite the Greek language and thought of the Orthodox Gospels and Pauline Epistles. "The Church may have grown up on Greek soil, but Christianity itself is not Greek in origin. The very earliest stage of all . . . is not Greek but Semitic."[4] The reason for the lack of much important information about the ministry of Jesus is due to the Roman-Jewish war that culminated in the destruction of Jerusalem." The Jewish state came to an end, and with it perished the primitive Semitic Christianity. . . . Between the Church of the second century and the Apostles there is a great gulf fixed. . . ."[5]

He believes that we can begin to fill this void by turning our attention to "a strangely neglected branch of the Church. . . . I speak, of course, of the Christianity of the Euphrates valley, of the Church whose language was Syriac. . . . For the inner character of Syriac speaking Christianity in its early stages we must turn . . . to the surviving documents." This Syriac literature was discovered in the great Monophysite library of the Convent of S. Mary Deipara in the Nitrian desert.[6] Burkitt is convinced that the Syriac *Acts of Thomas* is immensely important for the history of Christian thought. It is one of the oldest works in Syriac literature. Despite evidence of redaction, quotations from Scripture are in original form. But it is certainly an unorthodox interpretation concludes Burkitt because no orthodox catholic author would present Judas Thomas as the twin brother of Jesus. . . . "No wonder that some of the manuscripts have obliterated this from the title!"[7]

The ideas in the *Acts of Thomas* focus on human nature and the concern is with the conversion of individual souls, not in the establishment of the Church. It is a "natural religion" or a "philosophy" that express a kind of Gnosticism rather than Catholicism.[8] However, Burkitt notes the strong ascetic character of this document that is quite contrary to the Western style of thinking and living. But even more important, there are selections we will present that do not seem to fit well with Jesus' gospel of a healthy, self-actualized life style.

Now, let us look at some of the details in the story of Thomas and Jesus in India. We begin with an account of Jesus and his friends in Syria.[9] The following is Benjamin's translation:

> And when all the apostles had been for a time in Jerusalem . . . they divided the countries among them, in order that each one of them might preach in the region which fell to him. . . . India fell by lot and division to Judas Thomas the Apostle. . . .[10]

But Thomas protests, citing his inability to speak the Indian language and lack of strength for the journey. However, Jesus is finally able to persuade him to make the trip.

One day, Jesus encounters a merchant, Habban by name, who has been sent by the earlier identified King Gudnaphar (Gandaphorus in the Internet translation) to hire a carpenter for the King's new building project. Jesus tells him he has a slave who is a carpenter, and he will sell him. Now, this is a very difficult part of the story for when have we ever heard of Jesus as a slaveholder? The very idea is completely at variance with Jesus' profound conviction that we are all children of God called to live in obedience to God alone. However, we can view this story from a pragmatic perspective. We have learned that Jesus had a gift for devising and acting out dramas to achieve a desired result. What better way to obtain money for the missionary journey and explain why he would travel to India with his former slave? After all, he also was a carpenter-craftsman who could offer his services to the monarch. The merchant agreed to pay twenty pieces of silver for Judas Thomas and Jesus wrote a bill of sale.

> I, Jesus, son of Joseph the Carpenter, from the village of Bethlehem, which is in Judea, acknowledge that I have sold my slave Judas Thomas to Habban, the merchant of King Gudnaphar'. . . .[11]

> And, he (Thomas) went to Habban the Merchant, without carrying anything with him except that price of his, for our Lord had given it to him. And Judas went and found Habban the merchant carrying his goods on board the ship, and began to carry them on board with him. . . . And they began to sail because the breeze was steady; and they were sailing along gently, until they put in at the town of Sandaruk.

They sailed on to Taxila and met the King who was celebrating the marriage of his daughter. He must have gained respect for them not only as skilled craftsmen but also as devout holy men for they were invited to attend the wedding festivities, and Thomas sang songs of praise to God. He was even asked by the King to bless his daughter and the groom in the bridal chamber after which Thomas leaves.

> The bridegroom raised the curtain that he may bring the bride to himself, and he saw our Lord standing and talking with the bride. And

the bridegroom said to him, "Lo, thou didst go out, and how art thou
still here?" Our Lord said to him, "I am not Judas, *but I am the
brother of Judas*" And our Lord sat down on the bed and let the
young couple sit on the chairs.[12] (Emphasis added)

This interesting little pericope makes two very interesting points. First, and
most important for our hypothesis of Jesus in India; the story plainly states that
Jesus is in India with Thomas at the princesses' wedding. In the second place,
Jesus is mistaken for Thomas because they look so much alike. The synoptic
account of Jesus' family does indeed include Judas as one of Jesus' three brothers but no Thomas is mentioned.[13] But, in the title of the source we are using,
Thomas has also the name Judas and that certainly identifies Thomas as Jesus'
brother because Jesus said, I am the brother of Judas. Moreover, the recently
discovered *Gospel of Thomas* identifies him as *didymos* or "the twin." The Prologue to the *Gospel of Thomas* begins as follows: "These are the secret sayings
that the *living Jesus* spoke and Didymos Judas Thomas recorded."[14] (Emphasis
added)

When we put all this material together, we conclude that Jesus had a twin
brother Judas Thomas, that would explain their identical features and the
groom's confusion. Of course, this also raises some serious theological problems
for those who hold the dogma of Jesus' virgin birth. Thomas must also have
been virgin born! After all, he was Jesus' twin. Would that make Thomas also a
divine person? I must confess, that I believe that the argument that Jesus had a
twin brother is stronger than the dogma or doctrine of Jesus' unique virgin birth
or more accurately, virgin conception.

But there is another problem with this Syriac text that we must address. A
careful reading reveals a subtext that I will call an overlay text. We have been
following Benjamin's argument that the Syriac text offers proof that Jesus was
in India with twin brother Thomas. I find no good reason to dispute this conclusion. However, the subtext or overlay text is challenging. At the very beginning
of the story there is a passage that suggest a late Christological theme. When
Thomas refuses to go to India, "the Saviour appears unto him by night and saith
to him; 'Fear not, Thomas, go thou unto India and preach the word there, for my
grace is with thee."[15]

Later in the story when Thomas is with the young bride and groom, he offers this prayer, "My Lord and my God, that travellist with thy servants . . . Jesus Christ, Son of compassion and perfect saviour, Christ, Son of the living God.
. . . I beseech thee, Lord Jesus, and offer unto thee supplication for these young
persons, that thou wouldest do for them the things that shall help them. . . . And
he laid his hands on them and said: The LORD shall be with you. . . ."[16]

Now both of these passages refer to a resurrected and living Christ; not to a
living human brother. There is no disputing that. But I suggest that we follow
Burkitt's line of reasoning that the Syriac text contains some very ancient and
historically accurate material about the twin brothers, Jesus and Judas Thomas,
embarking on a missionary journey to India. Since, we cannot deny the Chris-

tological passages, we must conclude that these are later redactions. New Testament scholars are very familiar with these layered texts, and they argue about which portions are oldest and most authentic.

Another textual problem concerns Jesus' response to Thomas' prayer. He begins his instruction to the bride and groom with these words.

"Remember, my children, . . . that if ye abstain from this foul intercourse, ye become holy temples, . . . and ye will acquire no cares of life or of children, whose end is destruction, . . . for they will be caught either in adultery or murder or theft or fornication, and by all these will ye be afflicted. . . . But if ye be persuaded and keep your souls chaste before God, there will come unto you living children whom these blemishes touch not, and ye shall be without care, leading a tranquil life without grief or anxiety, looking to receive that incorruptible and true marriage, and ye shall be therein groomsmen entering into the bride chamber which is full or immortality and light."[17]

Burkitt is quite right to identify these passages as of Gnostic origin. A persistent Gnostic theme proclaims that we are all fallen souls, condemned to live in this evil world. Only the Savior's teaching about our condition and obedience to his command to live celibate lives that are free from sex and procreation will bring about our salvation. Then we shall be released from this evil world to rise up to our heavenly home.

Jesus, a Jew, could never have spoken the words quoted above. A primary theme of Judaism is that our good God made a good world in which we are to learn to love God and one another, marry and beget children. There is certainly nothing evil about marriage and sex. It is obvious that these Gnostic texts are another example of late redaction. It is just as clear to me, that such examples of redaction do not invalidate the truth of the basic text about Jesus and brother Judas Thomas going on a missionary journey to India.

The next literary evidence that Benjamin introduced to support the belief that Jesus traveled to India is the *Bhavishya Mahapurana*, volume nine of eighteen volumes. Composition began in the 5th century B.C.E. and was translated from the original Sanskrit into English in 1910. Benjamin includes a photocopy of the beautiful Sanskrit script and an English translation. The part that interests us tells about King Shalivahana who ruled Kashmir and northwest India from 39-50 C.E.

> One day Shalivahana came to one of the high peaks of the Himalayas. There in the land of the Hun (Ladakh) the mighty King saw a noble person of white complexion wearing white garments.
>
> The King asked the holy man who he was and he replied cheerfully, "I am known as the Son of God, and born of a virgin!" He further said, "I am the exponent of the Mleacha dharma and preach truth!"
>
> Having heard this, the King asked, "What is your religion?"

He said, "O great King, I come from a foreign country where there is no
longer truth and where evil knows no bounds. I appeared as the messiah
in the land of Amalekites. But Ihamasi of the barbarians appeared in a
terrible form. Then having overcome their evil deeds, I became their
Messiah."

"O King, listen, the religion I established among the non-believers purified their souls and their bodies of dirt and superstition. After seeking
refuge in the prayers of the Naigama (a holy book or a form of Yoga),
man will pray to the Eternal. Through justice, truth, unity of spirit and
meditations, man will find his way to Issa (Jesus' name in India), in the
center of light. God the omnipotent and steadfast as the sun will unite
the spirit of all wandering beings in himself.

Thus, O King, Ihamasi will be destroyed and the pure image of Issa, the
giver of happiness will remain forever in the heart, and I was called
Issa-Masih (Messiah)!"

Having heard this, the King returned after making obeisance to him.[18]

This piece of evidence should be regarded as strong for several reasons.
King Shalivahana, who claimed to have encountered Jesus in Kashmir and
northwest India, ruled during the time period that Jesus could very reasonably
have been living—39 to 50 C.E. The description of Jesus as having a light com-
plexion would distinguish him from the relatively dark skinned people of the
region and the description of a white garment suggests the kind of clothing worn
in the Essene community to which Jesus may have belonged.

Some of the details of the message given to the King are also confirmation.
Issa says he has come from the land of the Amalekites—one of several names
for the region of Palestine—where much suffering has been brought by Ihamasi
(Satan) by way of the barbarians. It is not too much of a stretch to read Romans
here. His concluding remark about "having overcome their evil deeds" strongly
suggests Jesus' escape from death on the cross. The summary given of his teachings appears to closely resemble his compassionate ministry of healing the body
and freeing the mind of legalistic religion. The reference to truth, justice, and the
goal of spiritual union with the Eternal that will bring happiness to all people,
fits perfectly with Jesus' teachings, as the word "blessed" in the beatitudes,
makarias means "happy" in New Testament Greek.

But what are we to make of Jesus identifying himself as "known as the Son
of God, and born of a virgin"? In the synoptic gospels, Jesus always refers to
himself as a "son of man," that is, just another human person. The phrase "Son
of God" reflects a much later theology. The incident we are discussing occurred
during King Shalivahana's reign, sometime between 39 and 50 C.E. The reference to a virgin birth raises the same problems. Certainly, Jesus never said he
was virgin born and only the gospels of Matthew and Luke contain this tradition,

and they were probably not composed before 80 C.E. though the tradition could be earlier.

It would seem that this story about Jesus and the King exhibits signs of later redaction to reflect the developing theology about Jesus. But as we noted above, this should not diminish the importance of this tradition any more than should the gospel stories be discounted that contain evidence of much later redaction. Of course, it is possible that this incident occurred near the end of Jesus' life when he was leaving Palestine for the last time. He would have shared with his friends all that he had taught and learned in his Eastern journeys and would have been amazed to learn of the developing Christ cult doctrines that he had been virgin born and regarded as Son of God! On this interpretation, his language was ironic but he was powerless to stop such fantastic thinking. Besides, what he had shared with his friends was much more important and, as we will expound in a later chapter, would constitute the very core of the Fourth Gospel.

Jesus told the King that he was a teacher of the Mleacha dharma. In Sanskrit the word *mlec-cha* refers to a non-Indian barbarian of any race or culture or a class of untouchables comprised of such persons.[19] How very like Jesus to be so honest about himself using self-deprecating humor. In the next chapter, we will learn of the arguments that Jesus had with the elitist class of Brahmins about dividing God's children into levels of worth and how he quite boldly began preaching to the Sudras and Untouchables, something that Mahatma Gandhi was to do much later with the admission that he had been much influenced by the Jesus tradition.

We will conclude this chapter by remarking that Benjamin's scrupulous research using *The Acts of Judas Thomas* and Volume Nine of the *Bhavishya Mahaqurana* has provided very strong support for the belief that Jesus undertook a missionary journey to India after escaping death by crucifixion. We will now turn to the testimony of other scholars to strengthen the tradition that Jesus traveled, not only in India, and Kashmir but also to Persia and Tibet and perhaps even to China.

Chapter Five
Bodhisattva in Tibet with the Buddhists

Elizabeth Clare Prophet presents us with a very complete study of the traditions and legends about Jesus' travels in India, Kashmir, and Tibet in her well documented book, *The Lost Years of Jesus*. However, her understanding is quite different from our own. She believes that the traditions about Jesus in the East are about the young Jesus' journey to India, Kashmir, and Tibet, *before* he began his Palestinian and final Ministry. But in the light of other traditions, I began to wonder if perhaps she had it backwards. I now believe that the several traditions that we will consider in this chapter are about Jesus' *post*-Palestinian ministry as we argued in the last chapter. We will discover internal evidence that supports both theories but I will argue that the *post*-Palestinian ministry theory is the more convincing.

Nicolas Notovich, notes Clara Prophet, traveling in central Asia in the late nineteenth century, came to a monastery in Mulbekh that Prophet identifies as the gateway to the world of Tibetan Buddhism. There, a lama informed him that the archives at Lhasa, capital of Tibet and home of the Dalai Lama, contained many ancient scrolls about Issa, the Eastern name for Jesus. He was told that the greatest monasteries had copies of these manuscripts. He journeyed to one of them, Himïs, where the chief lama produced two volumes from which he read stories about Issa that Notovich copied into his journal. These notes were later published in his book *The Life of Saint Issa, Best of the Sons of Men*. It consisted of 224 verses summarizing Hebrew history from the Exodus to the Roman invasion and conquest. The rest describes Issa's travels in India and his study of the Vedas with Brahmin teachers. He aroused the wrath of the priestly caste when he tried to teach the common people and fleeing for his life, he journeyed to the birthplace of Sidhartha Gautama (the Buddha) in Nepal where he studied the Buddhist scriptures for six years. The remainder of the book concerns Jesus' ministry in Palestine. It is interesting and significant that there is no mention of the resurrection though Jesus is imprisoned, tried, and crucified. The empty tomb is mentioned concluding with the rumor "that the supreme Judge had sent his angels to carry away the mortal remains of the saint in whom dwelt on Earth a part of the Divine Spirit."[1]

Notovich's book was an immediate success in 1894. Many editions were published in French, English, German, Italian, Spanish, and Swedish. However, criticisms soon began to come in. The Russian author was charged with making up the entire story and many began to doubt that he had even made his journey to India and Tibet. Strong arguments from the eminent scholars Edgar J. Goodspeed and Max Müller must be faced. In Goodspeed's words: "On the whole, as an ancient document, the *Life of Issa* is altogether unconvincing. It reads more like the journalistic effort to describe what might have happened if Jesus had visited India and Persia in his youth and what a modern cosmopolite thinks he did and taught in his ministry in Palestine."[2]

Here are some of Goodspeed's objections:

The manuscript was not translated by a competent scholar but read by the lama while the interpreter translated and Notovich took notes.

Why did not Notovich go back to Tibet to confirm his discovery?

Why can we not find the sixty-three manuscripts that a Roman Catholic Cardinal told Notovich were in the Vatican Library?

Max Müller added the following criticisms:

The *Life of Issa* does not appear in the catalogue of the Tandjur and the Kandjur that contains great collections of Tibetan literature.

This story was learned from Jewish merchants who came to India immediately after the Crucifixion. How could they have come to know about Issa "among the uncounted millions of India"?[3]

We will address these criticisms as we acquaint ourselves with additional evidence of Jesus missionary journey in India that closely parallels that recorded by Notovich.

The next supporting evidence was provided by Nicholas Roerich who from 1924 to 1925 led an expedition through Central Asia to Tibet.[4] He was an internationally acclaimed artist and Prophet includes some of his truly magnificent paintings of Tibet in her book. He was a professor at the Imperial Archaeological Institute in Russia and was very interested in the tradition about Jesus in the East. His son George who accompanied him had studied Persian, Sanskrit, Chinese, and Tibetan at Harvard and the School of Oriental Languages in Paris. He published *Trails to Inmost Asia* in 1931. Nicholas, his father, authored *Altai-Himalaya*, and included many folk traditions that he heard about Jesus' adventures in Tibet. From one of the ancient manuscript that he dates as about 1500 years old (4th C.E.) he quotes: "Issa secretly left his parents and . . . turned towards Ind (India) to become perfected in the Divine Word, and for the study of the laws of the Great Buddha."[5]

Roerich visited Himïs and came to believe, through the disclosure of reticent details, that the lamas there had heard and knew about the Issa manuscripts. The many stories he had collected during his travels in many Asian lands corroborated their existence. Moreover, when we compare the texts obtained by Notovich and Roerich, we find that in ten of the chapters, sixty verses exactly correspond. This suggests a common original source and reminds us how New Testament scholars "discovered" the lost gospel of "Q", the sayings source of Jesus, though the original has never been found. Prophet notes that "without question, Professor Roerich believed the texts were authentic."[6] She also tells us that the eminent scholar of Tibetan literature, Lama Lobzang Mingyer Dorge was a member of the expedition. Surely, he would not have allowed his friend Nicholas to publish what he believed were spurious manuscripts.[7] It is noteworthy that Roerich was never attacked by the press, theologians, or scientists. While Edgar Goodspeed did dismiss Notovich's claims as unconvincing, he never mentioned Professor Roerich's more recent investigation.

This answers Goodspeed's complaint that Notovich never returned to Tibet to verify his claim. Roerich did it for him. Goodspeed's suspicion that the texts had not been expertly translated is answered by noting the several chapters in which sixty-six verses exactly correspond with the independent translations of Notovich and Roerich. His final objection that the documents could not be found in the Vatican library should not be too difficult to explain when we realize how very powerful this material is in a theological sense. What this theory would accomplish would be nothing less than revolutionary for, not only Roman Catholic but most orthodox and main stream Christianity. We shall have more to say of this later.

Max Müller's point about the manuscript not being included in the catalog of Tibetan literature was answered by Notovich who explained that the story about Issa was not recorded in a single volume. Müller's puzzlement to know about the mysterious Jewish merchants who just happened to know about Issa fits perfectly with the story about Jesus and Thomas going to India as recorded in the Syriac version of the Acts of Thomas that we earlier noted.

Another argument that accused Notovich of creating a fictional document came from a *Times* article about J. Archibald Douglas, Professor of Government College, Agra, India, who claimed to have journeyed to Himis and interviewed the Chief Lama there about the mysterious manuscript. He came away convinced by the Chief Lama that no such document existed.[8] But in response, Tibetologist Snellgrove and Skorupski published *The Cultural Heritage of Ladekh* in which they explained that the monks were very suspicious of Westerners who show undue interest in their manuscripts fearing they may want to steal them as had often happened.[9] This could explain the Chief Lama's denial about the existence of the manuscript.

Now we turn to the material recorded by Notovich in his *The Life of Saint Issa*

Chapter I
1. The Earth has trembled and the heavens have wept because of a great crime which has been committed in the land of Israel.
2. For they have tortured and there put to death the great and just Issa, in whom dwelt the soul of the universe.
3. Which was incarnate in a simple mortal in order to do good to man and to exterminate their evil thoughts.

The fact that the crucifixion is included in this story about Jesus' Eastern Ministry argues strongly that this material could not be about Jesus' early life, before his Palestinian ministry. The Incarnation theology is reminiscent of that found in John's gospel and Paul's letters and suggests that this material dates from the late first century, possibly 100 C.E. or later. While this late redaction could not be part of the details of Jesus' Eastern Ministry, it does not effect the authenticity of Notovich's gospel any more than do reactions in the canonical Gospels and the Acts of Thomas.

Chapters II and III present a very brief account of Israel's enslavement in Egypt and their deliverance by the pharaoh's son Prince Mossa (Moses) after a terrible pestilence decimated the Egyptians. There is no Passover story about God slaying the oldest Egyptian children and animals. Since the Qur'an does not include this ghastly story either, one wonders if perhaps Muhammad had access to this tradition. Then, the Israelites turned from God and suffered punishment from their enemies. It is interesting to note that it is not Babylon but Rome "on the other side of the sea" that, once again, makes slaves of them. As in the Deuteronomic formula, when Israel repents, God hears and forgives. It is quite reasonable that Jesus would have included this abbreviated version of Israel's history in his Eastern Ministry.

Chapter IV repeats the story of God's incarnation in a human being so that people can achieve moral purity and enter into the kingdom of heaven. A poor family gave birth to the divine child who was named Issa (Jesus) and amazed all who came to hear him speak. ". . . They marveled at the discourses proceeding from his childish mouth." (v. 9) As we noted earlier, this kind of story, not found in the canonical gospels but only in the much later apocryphal gospels cannot be attributed to Jesus. The next two verses tell us that by age thirteen, when marriages are arranged, many thronged about the house of Jesus hoping to gain him as a son-in-law. But, young Jesus had other interests and secretly left home to journey to India, "With the object of perfecting himself in the Divine World and of studying the laws of the great Buddha." (v. 13) Our theory would argue that Jesus' post crucifixion Eastern Ministry had to be disguised to avoid Roman retaliation. The story that Jesus traveled to India to avoid an arranged marriage achieved the desired intent, but is, of course, pure fiction.

Chapter V tells us about Issa's journey to India and how he impressed all who heard him. The Jains, especially wanted him to stay with them. This last could be explained in terms of Jesus' teachings about non-violence found in our canonical gospels. That would fit perfectly and may even have been a derivative of Jain/ Buddhist teachings that some scholars believe were known to the Essenes. He traveled on and lived for a while with "the white priests of Brahma " who taught Jesus to read the Vedas, and to heal by prayer. (V.3) But, during this six year sojourn with the Brahmins, he turned to teaching the lower castes (varnas), Vaisyas (merchants), and Shudras (farmers & workers), and was chastised by the elite Brahmins (priests) and Kshatriyas (soldiers). Vaisyas are permitted to hear the Vedas on festival days only, and the Shudras were forbidden even then because they are fated to be slaves to all for as long as they lived. "Death only can set them free from their servitude." (v. 9)[10]

Now, we have reached that part of the story about Jesus in India where we will begin to hear the sayings attributed to Jesus. Jesus rebelled against his aristocratic teachers and the elitist teachings of the Vedas. "God, the Father, makes no difference between his children: all to him are equally dear." (v. 11) He rejected the divine authority of the Vedas—at least those portions that denied human equality in God's eyes. It should not surprise us that Jesus turns from the kind of Brahmanism he had encountered to the more inclusive and compassionate way of the Buddha.

The Brahmins must have taught Jesus their doctrine of Trimurti, the three bodies of Brahman. This is a Trinitarian model of Indian theism closely resembling the Christian Trinity that would be developed three centuries later. The Trimurti, discloses the activity of Brahman (Ultimate Reality) in three modes: 1. Brahma: Personal Creator (God, the Father); Vishnu: Lord of the Moral Law, who incarnates as an Avatar, Descending One, and comes as Savior (God the Son); and Shiva, Lord of the Dance of the processing universe (God, the Holy Spirit). But to Jewish Jesus, this would have sounded like tri-theism, and he could not accept Trinitarian theology even in this modalist form. He replies:

15. The Judge Eternal, the Eternal Spirit, comprehends the one and indivisible Soul of the universe, which alone creates, contains, and vivifies all.
16. He alone has willed and created, he alone has existed since all eternity, and his existence will have no end. He has no equal either in the heavens or on Earth.

Three theological points become clear in these passages. First and foremost, Jesus proclaims the unqualified monotheism of his Jewish faith. He will tolerate no compromise here. The Trimurti (Trinity) of Brahmanism must be rejected because of its tritheistic implications. Pantheism, the idea that Brahman—The Holy Power—resides in all things, animate and inanimate, Jesus also rejects because to include the imperfections of Creation in the divine nature would compromise the perfect power, wisdom, and goodness of God. Jesus surely held the traditional Jewish belief that God is intimately related to every part of nature without being nature.

Chapter VI tells us about Jesus' flight from the "white priests and warriors" aided by the Sudras, and how he journeyed to the homeland of Sidhartha Buddha in northeast India in the company of the Buddhists who were beginning to flee persecution by the dogmatic and elitist Brahmins. Having become acquainted with the compassionate, non-violent lifestyle of the Buddhists, he would have been quite ready to join their company in India.

3. After having perfected himself in the Pali language, the just Issa applied himself to the study of the sacred writings of the Bud-

dhist Sutras. After studying for six years, he began preaching
again, "that we should do good to our neighbors if we would
draw close to God."
11. "Even as a Father would act towards his children, so will God
judge man after their deaths according to the laws of his mercy.
Never would he so humiliate his child as to transmigrate his
soul, as in a purgatory, into the body of an animal."

Two theological issues are here. First, Jesus teaches the double commandment that loving God is inseparable from loving our neighbors and second, he
rejects the view of transmigration that teaches persons might be reincarnated as
beasts as inconsistent with his experience of God as loving Parent.

We have noted that the earliest kind of Buddhism was atheistic, but I prefer
the non-judgmental term, non-theistic Buddhism. These Theravadan Buddhists
adopted a strict empirical (almost positivist) way of viewing the self in the
world. Their reductionist analysis of a person discovered five skandas or
"heaps" that together constitute a person. There is the material body with it's
sense preceptors, linked with the physical brain that produces sensations, consciousness, and volition. The idea of an independent and immortal self or soul is
an illusion.[11] This analysis and conclusion sounds very much like modern
physiological psychology and epiphenomenalism, that also denies the reality of
mind or soul as an independent entity. Such thinking is the basis of much research to develop artificial intelligence (A.I.).

The Buddhist term *anatman* or no *atman* or soul would infuriate Hindus
who believed that Brahman was the cosmic Soul or Atman of all that is. It must
have also seemed absurd to Jesus for whom his personal God and the created
community of persons was at the center of his faith. I can imagine Jesus engaging in numerous debates about the necessary reality of atman or soul. He certainly must have challenged the Theravadins to explain how their wonderful
spirit of compassion (*karuna* love) and friendliness (*meta* love) could be finally
grounded in nothing more than the *sva laksanas* and *dharmas* (atomic realities)
that swirreled eternally in the mindless cosmic process of *anicca*.[12]

Today, some philosophers would use the term unconscious axiogenisis or
the mindless and accidental creation of value to describe such a philosophy. Of
course, if one is a materialist or naturalist or logical positivist, that is exactly
what to believe. But what evidence do we find that unconscious process ever
created anything? The Theravadins would answer that the entire universe is the
answer. But that argument fails on the charge of "question begging." That is, the
conclusion is not "earned" but "begged" from the premise that was already believed to be true without any supporting evidence. On the other hand, theists
support their argument with numerous examples of ideas, literature, philosophy,
objects of art and technology, that have all been the product of conscious mind.
And so the argument continues to this day.[13]

But Jesus was no philosopher, and he must have stressed, above all philosophy and scripture, his own overwhelming personal experience of encountering

the Father-like personal God, not only at his baptism but also throughout his life. Moreover, Jesus was widely recognized as the living example of a God-filled man. His Indian name Issa means saint or lord. Finally, this kind of argument, though supported by good reasons, must be decided by faith. Some may prefer to use Kierkegaard's term "leap of faith." In any case, I would hope it would be *reasonable* faith and not the insane faith of some fanatical believers that leads to violence. When asked to perform a miracle to support his teaching about the existence of God, we read the words of Issa.

> 4.   The miracles of our God have been worked since the first day when the universe was created: they take place every day and at every moment. Whosoever seeth them not is deprived of one of the fairest gifts of life.

This kind of argument of God's existence reminds us of Paul's argument in his letter to the Romans that invited his readers to ponder the order of nature as a powerful argument for God's existence.[14] Today, theologians would call this the cosmological argument for God that appeals to our intuited belief that all created things in nature must have an adequate cause. Such reasoning from experience would appeal to the logical, empirically-minded Buddhists. But, of course, this would also be a powerful challenge to their non-theism. They had already argued with the Brahmins about this and now, here was Jesus adding fuel to the fire.

At this point, the manuscript tells us that Jesus traveled west and entered Persia preaching his gospel of loving communion with God. Now, it is the Zoroastrian priests who are offended and arrest him for interrogation. In Chapter VIII, we read:

> 4.   Of what new God dost thou speak? Art thou not aware, unhappy man, that Saint Zoroastor is the only just one admitted to the privilege of communion with the Supreme Beings, . . ?

The verses that follow have Jesus admonishing them not to worship the sun. This, of course, was not the original religion of Zoroaster or Zarathustra. Fire was the symbol of deity as it had been in many cultures for countless centuries. But, some religions seem to lose sight of their original pure monotheism and so it was with Zoroastrianism. The original pure monotheism eventually became so distorted that a dualistic interpretation evolved in which Ahura Mazada or Spenta Mainyu was the Good God of Light and Andra Mainyu or Ahriman was the Evil God of Darkness. Jesus admonishes them:

> 17.   The Eternal Spirit is the Soul of all that is animate. You commit a great sin in dividing it into a spirit of evil and a spirit of good, for there is no God outside the good, . . .
> 18.   Who, like unto the father of a family, does but good to his children, forgiving all their faults if they repent them.

20. Wherefore, I say unto you, Beware of the day of judgment, for
God will inflict a terrible chastisement upon all those who shall
have led his children astray from the right path and have filled
them with superstitions and prejudices. . . .

Jesus promised forgiveness for all who repent but warned of a day of judgment for those who teach false beliefs. The idea of a final judgment that sepa-
rates good people from evil does seem to have come from Zoroastrianism originally and was carried back to Jerusalem by Jewish exiles returning from Babylon and then absorbed into the theology of the Pharisees. Jesus teaches a version
of this doctrine, mercifully stripped of the ghastly Zoroastrian details about fire,
brimstone, and boiling lead for the damned!

The remaining chapters, IX-XIV, tell of Jesus' ministry in Palestine. We
read about the Roman occupation and the persecution of the Jews. Jesus traveled
among his people encouraging them to persevere and remain faithful to God.
Pilate, becoming alarmed at Jesus' growing popularity has him arrested, tried,
and crucified. He sends his soldiers to claim Jesus' body and bury it elsewhere,
fearing a popular uprising. The next day, the crowd found the tomb empty and a
rumor spread that god had sent an angel to carry Jesus' remains away. (This last
statement if modified to read "friends," "rescue," and "heal" would fit with the
interpretation we have developed.)

Now, contrary to the theory we have presented, all of this happened after
Jesus had studied and traveled in the East. In Chapter IX, we read: v.1. "Issa . . .
had reached his twenty-ninth year when he returned to the land of Israel."

If our theory is correct this statement is not true. Then, why would such a
false assertion arise? As earlier noted, the rather obvious answer is that to place
Jesus' ministry in India and Tibet *after* his Palestinian ministry would have
given away the truth of the failed crucifixion. The furious Romans would have
increased tormenting the Jews, especially Jesus' friends and family who knew
the truth about the Suffering Servant drama of Israel. This is why the false legend about Jesus going to the East *before* his adult ministry was contrived.

We now turn to Swami Abhedananda's translation of the ancient text of St.
Issa's adventures in India and Tibet to make a comparative study of his translation with that by Nicolas Notovich that we have just reviewed. Swami Abhedananda wanted to verify or falsify Notovich's claim and traveled to Tibet. There,
the lama at Himis verified Notovich's story, showed him the book about Issa,
and helped Swami Abhedananda translate the text. From this came his book, in
Kashmir and Tibet, that he coauthored in cooperation with his assistant
Bramachari Bhairav Chaitanya.[15] In 1954, Swami Prajnananda published a revised second edition. Abhedananda's interpretation of the ancient manuscript
almost exactly parallel's that of Notovich. Prophet notes that Abhedananda was
a friend of Max Müller and acquainted with his skeptical conclusion. In defense
of his positive evaluation, he notes "the chemistry between Abhedananda and
the lamas of Himis was entirely different than that between Notovich or Douglas
and the lamas. . . . He was a disciple of Rama Krishna. . . . He was too much a

kinsman and too perceptive to be taken in by any 'waggish monks' as Müller put it."[16]

Our summary of Abhedananda's gospel will focus only on portions that differ from that of Notovich. The opening chapters parallel those in Notovich's version. They are about the Incarnation (late redaction, earlier noted) and Israel's troubled history. Next, we read of Jesus' refusal to marry and his flight to India with a group of traders. In Chapter V, v. 2, we find an interesting description of Jesus' appearance.

> 2.   While traveling alone along the land of the five rivers (the Punjab), his majestic features, peaceful face, and broad forehead promoted the devoted Jains to recognize him as one who had received the mercy of the Lord.

Jesus learned Sanskrit from the Brahmins and studied the Vedas. He next journeyed to the birthplace of the Lord Buddha, learned the Pali language and studied Buddhist literature for six years. He then turned west and entered Persia, where he studied the teachings of Zoroaster. All of this parallels what we have earlier learned from Notovich's translation of the manuscript. Abhedananda adds a concluding note.

> The reverent lama said . . . three or four years after he (Jesus) left his body, the original manuscript was compiled in Pali from descriptions of all those Tibetians who met him at that time, as well as from descriptions of the traders who, with their own eyes, witnessed his crucifixion by the King of his country.[17]

This passage makes two valuable contributions to our critical analysis. We now know something about the authorship of the manuscript and the date of composition. The reference to the crucifixion drama—even eyewitnesses— supports our theory that all of this material about Jesus occurred *after* his Palestinian ministry. Of course, that would mean that the authors knew that Jesus had escaped death at the hands of his Roman executioners but as we explained earlier, this could not be divulged.

There is also a clue in Abhedananda's text that supports our theory that Jesus planned and acted out the Suffering Servant drama, including the rescue scene. In Chapter V, we read:

> 5.   In due course, he arrived at the home of Jagannath, the country of Vyasa-Krishna's mortal play. . . .

The footnote explains: "Mortal play describes the action of a god who plays a role—i.e., takes a mortal form, which begins with birth and ends with death— for a specific purpose, such as the incarnation of Krishna."[18] Is Abhedananda, through his interpreter, trying to suggest to his readers that he knows the secret of Jesus' final play? Or is he suggesting that, presuming he believes all this occurred *before* the Palestine ministry, that this is how and where Jesus got the idea? I believe it is the former and Abhedananda knows the truth but does not think it prudent to upset the 2000-year-old applecart of Christianity that "Jesus died for our sins." I will explain later why this should not deliver a fatal blow to our Christian faith.

We next examine the testimony of Nicholas Roerich, professor at the Imperial Archaeological Institute in Russia, who led an expedition through Central Asia and, as noted earlier, was accompanied by his son George who had studied Chinese, Persian, Sanskrit, and Tibetan languages at Harvard and the School of Oriental languages in Paris. Also in their company was the eminent scholar of Tibetan literature, Lama Lobzeng Mingyer Dorje. Here are some excerpts from *Altai-Himalaya, Heart of Asia and Himalaya, With original texts on Saint Issa.* Roerich begins his gospel with remarks that reveal his sensitivity to the feelings of the people who guard the tradition.

"Regarding the manuscript of Christ—first there was a complete denial. Of course, denial first comes from the circle of missionaries, (who would, of course, be propagating the traditional Resurrection theology). Then slowly, little by little, are creeping fragmentary reticent details, difficult to obtain. Finally it appears—that about the manuscript the old people in Ladak have heard and know."[19] "In Ladak, we again encountered the legend of Christ's visit to these parts. . . . We heard several versions of this legend which has spread widely throughout Ladak, Sinkiang, and Mongolia. . . . It is valuable to see that the legend is told in full sincerity."[20] Professor Roerich's testimony gains strength and credibility from the following statements about son George. "How wonderful that George knows all necessary Tibetan dialects. Only without a translator will people here speak about spiritual things."[21] "We learned how widespread are the legends about Issa. It is important only to know the substance of these legends. The sermons related in them, of unity, of the significance of women, and all the implications about Buddhism, are so remarkably timely for us. . . . Appreciate how close to contemporary consciousness is the substance of the legends and be astonished how widely all the East knows of them and how persistent is the repetition of them."[22]

Two factors count in favor of believing that there is an ancient text containing stories about Saint Issa (Jesus) in the monastery at Himis that was probably copied from the original in Lassa. First, as noted earlier, sixty of the verses in the document that Professor Roerich independently produced are parallels to the document that was earlier translated for Nicolas Notovich. It is simply not reasonable to suppose that a deliberate hoax could have been duplicated so precisely more than twenty-five years later. Secondly, Professor Roerich's son George was knowledgeable in the language of Pali in which the manuscript was written and also fluent in several Tibetan dialects spoken by the monks doing the translating. That would seem to put a hoax beyond the realm of credibility.

Some of the parallel sections referred to above include: the story of Jesus leaving home to journey to India to study the Vedas and the Sutras; how Jesus turned from the elitist Brahmanical teachings to teach the lowly Sudras because

God loves all classes of people; his compassionate teachings of neighbor love; his views that miracles abound in everyday living; that God is the Eternal Spirit beyond empirical discovery, that we must stop sacrificing animals and avoid superstitious religion; and that the prophets taught forgiveness, not revenge.[23] There are more parallels about Jesus' return to Palestine and his subsequent fall into disfavor with the religious and political authorities.

Here, again, is the problem regarding the date of composition. If these stories about Jesus were recorded *before* the Palestinian ministry, how could the author possibly have known about the conclusion of Jesus' ministry? If they were written after the final events in Jesus' life in Palestine then, of course, it would make perfect sense. But then, we would need to place the stories about Jesus' eastern ministry *after* his Palestinian ministry, which is what our theory is claiming. We have previously explained how the ruse of putting the stories *before* the Palestinian ministry conserves the fiction that Jesus died by crucifixion. Who would find this a valuable way to precede? The only reasonable answer is someone writing *after* fifty C.E. from the developing Christ Cult perspective that Paul was creating. Paul was preaching that Jesus' sacrificial death was the key to our salvation. But, remember that Paul was not living in Palestine during the Palestinian ministry and never knew Jesus, or, presumably, any of the members of his "play." We conclude that these stories about Jesus' eastern ministry, following his Palestinian ministry, are true.

We have been developing two major theories in this book. The first, is that Jesus survived the crucifixion in his faithful enactment of the Suffering Servant drama. Isaiah's and Jesus' great message to the suffering people of Israel was: do not despair, God will not forsake you, you will survive because God has great plans for you. We noted earlier in another of the Servant poems, Isaiah proclaimed that it is not enough for the Servant to restore the ancient kingdoms of Israel and Judah. The Servant must bring his vision of justice and peace to the ends of the Earth.[24] We suggested that this Servant poem inspired Jesus' missionary journey to the East. The first Servant Poem was about Servant Israel who suffers but is rescued. The second poem is about Servant Israel as Missionary to the world, and it is this second poem that Jesus has been acting out in the East. But in the course of learning about eastern religion and teaching his own gospel of God's love for us, Jesus made a profound impression on his hearers, especially the Buddhists.

Our second theme will be to show how the teachings we have just reviewed, that we accept as authentic teachings of Jesus in India and Tibet, helped to inspire an entirely new form of Buddhism. We noted that the earliest school of Buddhism was non-theistic Theravada; really more of a psychological philosophy than a religion. The teachings of Issa discovered by Notovich, Roerich and Swami Abhedananda contain clear statements about a loving personal God. Jesus' charismatic personality grounded in his powerful experience of his Father's presence must have deeply impressed the Buddhists. Certainly Jesus' emphasis on the boundless compassion of God would have fit perfectly with the Buddhist teachings of *karuna* compassion.

The Buddhists were already deeply involved in arguments with the Brahmins about theism. Unfortunately, their inclusion of animal sacrifice and their elitist view of humankind was a turn off. But Jesus' gospel of a compassionate heavenly Father who cherishes all of his children equally and who rejects sacrifice would have been gladly received by Jesus' Buddhist listeners. We propose that Jesus' witness added a powerful impetus to forces already working to move the northern branch of Buddhism to Mahayana theism. This theistic religious form of Buddhism would, in the centuries to follow, sweep across northern Asia, through Tibet, Mongolia, China, and into Japan. In asserting this, we are making a very large claim for the historical Jesus. Jesus will be seen as contributing to the founding of not one, but two world religions: Christianity and Mahayana Buddhism. He is both Christ and Bodhisattva! The terms Bodhisattva and Christ are, of course, titles and not proper names. They are used to identify a person or persons who most clearly reveal the highest spiritual value. For Christians, it would be the *agape* love of our Heavenly Father God. For Mahayana Buddhists, it would be the compassionate *karuna* love of the cosmic Buddha Mind.

To further develop our thesis for Jesus' ministry in the East, we turn our attention to another body of manuscripts that were discovered in China and recently re-translated by Martin Palmer, Director of the International Consultancy of Religion, Education, and Culture (ICOREC) and author of *The Jesus Sutras*.

Chapter Six
Ye Su in China with the Taoists

More evidence for Jesus' ministry in Asia is supplied by the newly translated *Jesus Sutras*. I first learned of them in Martin Palmers' book, wherein he explains that they had been brought by Bishop Aluban of the Syriac Church in Central Asia to the northwestern oasis town of Dunhuand, China, in the seventh century C.E. At that time, Taoism was the official religious philosophy of China, and the tolerant Tang Emperor received him graciously and gave the Christian missionaries permission to freely teach their gospel. Four centuries later (1065 C.E.), the hundreds of scrolls brought by the Bishop were placed in a Taoist/Buddhist monastery that was sealed and forgotten. Not until the end of the nineteenth century did a Taoist priest discover the library that had been cut into the side of a mountain. The Jesus Sutras were still there.

Palmer learned about them from studying a twelve foot high stone stele preserved in the Stone Steles Museum in Xian, China. The "stone sutras", as Palmer calls them, told of Bishop Aluban's visit and the Sutra Library in Dunhuand. In the course of an exciting adventure, he visited the library and began the task of translating them with the help of his skilled associates who were eminently qualified to translate from the Chinese and in the exegesis of Buddhist and Taoist concepts. Palmer was well qualified as he had earlier translated the *Tao te Ching* and the *Analects of Confucius*.

The Jesus Sutras contain material that is in the canonical gospels and also stories about Jesus' travels in India, Persia, and Tibet that we have already learned about. But now, we have evidence that Jesus also had a ministry in China. The Jesus Sutras have a unique oriental flavor that causes us to ask about authorship. Were they interpretations of Jesus' gospel by Buddhist and Taoist converts and scribes? Or do they go directly back to Jesus himself and reflect his own unique way of integrating oriental insights with his own Jewish beliefs? I am convinced of the truth of the latter because we have already seen how Jesus was able to accept some ideas from Brahmanism and Buddhism.

We turn now to examine what Palmer identifies as the Four Jesus Sutras and the Four Liturgical Sutras. We might call this the gospel of Palmer.

The First Sutra: The Sutra of the Teachings of the World Honored One.

This Sutra contains material that parallels the teachings of Jesus found in the Sermon on the Mount. Regarding prayer for forgiveness we read:

"Don't hesitate when you pray. Ask for forgiveness for your sins and at the same time forgive those who have sinned against you. The Heavenly Ruler above will forgive you as you forgive others." (Chapter One[1]) I suggest that this may very well be one of Jesus' most important sayings because it so unambiguously states that forgiveness is a reciprocal matter. The only way we can be forgiven is by offering forgiveness to others. This is completely at variance with the traditional view of the Atonement that we will receive forgiveness if we believe that the Son of God's blood sacrifice paid all our debts to God the Father. Jesus' teaching is ethical; the traditional formula is not. I bring this up because it is strong evidence of our thesis that Jesus never intended that his Suffering Servant drama be interpreted as a blood sacrifice. He did not *die* for our sins; he *lived* to teach us the way to being forgiven was to cultivate a loving relationship with our neighbors so that we might, with God, build a world community of justice, love, and peace.

Chapter Two contains more of Jesus' teachings including the Golden Rule. "Act toward others as you would have them act toward you. . . . Look for the best in others and correct what is worst in yourself."[2] The remaining chapters, three through seven, present material about Jesus' relationship to God and interesting details about the Crucifixion and Resurrection. Regarding Jesus' relationship to God, we will skip ahead to Chapter 4:11-16. "Anybody who says 'I am a god' should die. The Messiah is not the Honored One (God). Instead through his body (life) he showed the people the Honored One. . . . He showed love to all around him. . . ." This may be the best example we have in the Jesus Sutras that Jesus never claimed to be God! The theology of the God-man is a product of Western Christology. The words here attributed to Jesus sound more like the Nestorian two-nature Christology that Frederick Schlieremacher was much later to call the consciousness and dependence theory of the incarnation. To put it in modern language, Jesus was the God-filled man; always conscious of God's will for him and always faithful in his dependence on God's guidance. The above passage dramatically clarifies Jesus' teaching about himself, and it is perfectly compatible with his Jewish monotheistic faith.

Now, regarding the resurrection, we return to Chapter 3.

"The Jews trapped him, and he spoke of his understanding of who he really was. He said, 'I am the Messiah.' They said, 'How dare he say this! He is not the Messiah—not the true Messiah. He is mad and should be arrested. . . .' He was arrested and tried according to the strict law of the land, and hung up on high." (Ch. 3)[3] "While his Five Attributes passed away, he did not die but was released again after his death." (Ch. 4)[4] This is an enigmatic passage for our theory. Is it to be understood in the orthodox way, as a statement about his death and resurrection, or are we to read "death" euphemistically and "released" literally? Note also the unambiguous statement, "he did not die." The Five Attributes refer to the earlier noted Buddhist concept of the empirical person as body, sense preceptors, perceptions, conscious mind, and will. The language that they had passed away is consistent with the idea that Jesus had only lost consciousness but was still alive.

The Mahayana Buddhism that was emerging during the time of Jesus' ministry included a personalistic school that affirmed the existence of the self or soul (atman) the Buddhists call pudgala.[5] Even though the Five Attributes or Skandas failed, the pudgala survived. We can suggest that, on this interpretation, the quoted passage supports our thesis that Jesus did not die but was rescued. The following passage about Jesus visiting his disciples after the crucifixion ordeal underscores this conclusion. "He was with them for fourteen days in one month. Not a single day passed without them seeing him." "He came to them all at their place of prayer, so that his students, and then the whole world, should know the truth." From our perspective, the truth is that just as he had been rescued after suffering and was alive so suffering Israel will live to continue her missionary work in the world. (Ch, 5)[6]

Chapter Eight contains a Jesus saying that recalls how he broke with the aristocratic Brahmins and Kshatriyas in India and turned to teaching the lowly Sudras.

"The Messiah chose ordinary people to be his disciples. The true religion comes from Heaven, and I teach it. Know this. This is not the way of the Holy Founders and Kings. They choose their disciples from the rich and powerful, and control things through petty people." (Ch. 8)[7] These words express the same equalitarian spirit of Jesus that we find in the synoptic gospels.

The Second Sutra: The Sutra of Cause, Effect, and Salvation.

This Sutra contains a reference to the "Sacred Spirit" denied by the materialistic Theravada philosophers.

"Everything under Heaven has two natures. . . . The two natures are body and sacred spirit. . . . But the body only lives for a short time whilst the heavenly soul lives on in the power of the One Sacred Spirit and never decays." (Ch. 2)[8] The language clearly reflects the emerging Mahayana idealistic philosophy that finds expression in the above noted pudgala concept of an indwelling immortal soul. It would have been natural for Jesus to include his belief in an immortal soul, that he had shared with the Indian Buddhists, in his teachings to his new Chinese Buddhist/Taoist friends.

This idea is developed further in Chapter Three.

> The soul has Five Skandas. There is form, perception, consciousness, action, and knowledge. Everyone can see, hear, and speak. Without eyes you cannot see, without hands you cannot act, without feet you cannot walk. . . . The soul (pudgala) of a human being can only exist because of the Five Skandas. . . . Only by being clothed in the physicality of the Five Skandas can the soul savor the beauties and wonders of existence. The soul needs to be physically clothed.

Contrary to the Theravadin belief that body produces soul, the statement suggests that the soul has independent and primary existence and uses the physical bodily components as instrumental values. The reader will note that the

"Five Skandas" that comprise the empirical person are identified with different terms in the several traditions.

The end of Chapter Three and Chapter Four include interesting passages about karma, reincarnation and Heaven.

"The souls of the dead will once again be clothed by the Five Skandas. But this time, the Five Skandas will be perfected, needing no food to sustain them nor clothing to cover them. The souls will exist in complete happiness, untouched by physical needs. . . . Everything under Heaven feels happy. . . ." (Ch. 3)[9]

This passage clearly shows how Jesus' gospel dispels all fear of karma and reincarnation. However, this doesn't mean that Jesus rejected karma and reincarnation. Chapter Four, Verse Six, clearly states that "Whatever you do in life will have its karmic impact upon your soul and will affect the physical life of the soul." Furthermore, reincarnation is affirmed. "A person can only change his karma residue by being born again into the world." (v. 18) "Everyone's soul is eternal and is born into this changing, ephemeral world with its Skandas from the worldly womb. When we finally live good lives, we will escape to the world beyond this world." (4:19) Contrary to the theology of salvation by grace alone that Paul was developing back in the Roman world, the Jesus Sutras put much emphasis on works. "This world is the only place to decide your next birth. There is no other way forward—do good in this world to enter the next. It cannot be done otherwise." (Ch. 4:30-32)[10]

These ideas are straight out of Brahman-Buddhist thought. It would be interesting to know if they were imposed onto Jesus' gospel by redactors or if Jesus himself came to accept them and the Jesus Sutras are accurate reflections on his own thinking. I believe that the later is the case because Jesus' experience based faith was never closed minded, and I do not believe that he would be adverse to adopting and adapting new ideas as long as they were not inimical to his own lived relationship with his loving Heavenly Father. If reincarnation offered a way to come closer to God, Jesus would not have found it objectionable. Of course, from the perspective of orthodox Christianity, such thinking is unacceptable because it contradicts the idea that we have only one chance to be accepted by God, irrespective of our unequal situations in life. In offering persons additional chances to mature ethically and spiritually, reincarnation would seem to be consistent with a compassionate and reasonable deity. The philosophical problem lies in what I have called, in an earlier book, the "amnesia phenomenon." If we cannot recall our past lives with all the mistakes we have made, I argued, how are we going to be able to move ahead by learning from our past.[11] Believers answer that it is our *character*, and not our personal ego that survives, and our subconscious mind informs us of what we have achieved or failed to achieve in past lives. I confess that I have begun to appreciate the reasonableness of their belief, though I firmly believe that all ethical and spiritual experience must be grounded in the self-consciousness of an enduring person. The "amnesia phenomenon" could be explained as a temporary condition enabling reincarnated persons to begin a new experience free of overwhelming past traumatic episodes.

Chapters Five and Six admonish us to worship God alone and never worship ghosts. God is called the One Sacred Spirit and true worship will put us on the way to getting free from our sins. This sounds very much like conventional Christian theology especially when we read, "There was no other way to free us from sins but for Him to enter this world. So, He came and suffered a life of rejection and pain before returning." (Ch. 5:17, 18) I do not believe that these passages reflect Western theology, rather they are Jesus' way of explaining the role of the Suffering Servant Israel and the healing power of vicarious suffering that results in enlightenment. There certainly is not the slightest hint of an amoral blood sacrifice.

The Third Sutra: The Sutra of Origins

Palmer notes that this Sutra was purchased from China in the 1920s and is now in a Japanese private collection.[12] This Sutra tells us that "Every living thing comes from the One Sacred Spirit. Everything originates in the One Sacred Spirit. . . ." (Chapter One)[13] Chapter Two explains that humanity dwells between Heaven and Earth as is taught in the Taoist texts and Neo Confucianism. We have here a kind of Trinity wherein in humanity (headed by the Emperor) must live in harmony with the Earth and Heaven's norms.[14]

Probably the most noteworthy aspects of this Sutra are the ways in which Buddhist and Taoist ideas are integrated into the gospel story. For example, the Buddhist concept of Ultimate Reality as *Sunyata* or Void is used to refer to the Divine Mind. "The Great Holy Intelligence is as the Void: emptiness and thus invisible." (3:4) This suggests the Taoist teaching that Ultimate Reality or Tao is like an uncarved block before the sculpture begins to carve it into a specific shape. It is void or "devoid" of any specific form. It is, in fact, infinite potentiality. All is eternally proceeding from this Cosmic Womb and recycling back into It. Jesus would have grasped this ideas as relating to the second commandment. Compare "You shall make no graven images" (Exodus 20:4) with "The Tao that can be named is not the eternal Tao." (*Tao to King*, 1)

Again, we read, "The One Sacred Spirit simply is existing in *wu wei*, being in beinglessness and beyond touch. . . . The One Sacred Spirit is uncreated and is the essence of all existence and can never be emptied." (3:12-18) *Wu wei* is, of course, the golden rule of Taoism. Literally, it means "no action" or "doing by nondoing." In an ethical sense, it guides us to live authentically by avoiding all unnecessary and especially unnatural actions. That idea would fit very well with Jesus' teachings about the flowers who "neither spin nor weave" and yet are gloriously attired! In a metaphysical sense, God, The One Sacred Spirit, creates and sustains all—the entire universe—by just being the Ground of All Being—to use Tillich's phrase. "The One Sacred Spirit is uncreated and is the essence of all existence and can never be emptied." (3:18)

The Fourth Sutra: The Sutra of Jesus Christ

Compelling evidence that this is authentic Jesus material based on Jesus' ministry in China is found in his non-vindictive teachings and sayings that stress having a sensitive and compassionate attitude toward others less fortunate. "Do not bully those weaker than you. . . . If someone is hungry, even if he is your enemy, care for him, forgive and forget. . . . Do not laugh at poor people in rags and tatters. Do not obtain anything by deception or force" (4:27-39) Jesus' teachings based on agape (ethical love) are so similar to Gautama's teachings based on Karuna (compassionate love) and Lao Tzu's wu wei (reverential love) for the way of Nature, that they would find complete acceptance by his Buddhist/Taoist listeners.

Chapter Five contains a brief summary of Jesus' life using his Chinese name, Ye Su.[15] The story of his arguments with the scholars, as his enemies are called, and the crucifixion is recounted. But there is no statement that he died or was resurrected. Strangely, reminiscent of Mark's lost ending, the Fourth Jesus Sutra also breaks off. "As a result. . . ." (5:52) The thought is not completed. Could the reason for this lost ending be the same as that we postulated concerning the last ending of Mark? Later missionaries of Roman Christianity would have had good reason to suppress the story of Jesus' survival and continuing ministry.

Palmer identifies four more Sutras that he calls the great Liturgical Sutras. He observed that "One core concept that shapes all the liturgical Sutras is that of original nature. This is radically at variance with traditional Christian thought, which has tended to emphasize the deficits of humanity: the fault of original sin."[16] We earlier observed that the idea of a loving parent God who would condemn countless numbers of her/his children to Hell because of the disobedience of the first couple is completely unacceptable from an ethical point of view. It is certainly an absolute contradiction of Jesus' love ethos. The idea of original goodness or virtue was posited by Meng tzu (Mincious) the greatest disciple of Kung fu tzu (Confucious). Jesus would certainly be in agreement with this concept that he would also have found implied in the teachings of Gautama Buddha.

This idea is fully developed in the *Third Liturgical Sutra: the Sutra of Returning to Your Own Original Nature*. The first two chapters are a Taoist understanding of the Sermon on the Mount in which Ye Su (Jesus) instructs Simon (Peter) about following the Way of Triumph to the place of Peace and Happiness. (1:11-13)[17] Chapters Three and Four further this discourse but it is in Chapter Five that we discover the Four Essential Laws or Ways of the Dharma that are so Taoist in tone that we might call them the Tao of Jesus. These are the rules that can lead us back to our Original Goodness.

The Four Essentials Law of the Dharma: (the Buddhist term for moral law and duty).

> The First is No Wanting or the Way of No Desire.
> The Second is No (artificial) Doing. Don't put on a mask and pretend to be what you are not. Be your most natural (self). . . . So walk the Way of No Action.

The Third is No Piousness. And what that means is not wanting to have your good deeds broadcast to the nation. . . . This is the Way of No Virtue.

The Fourth is No Dogmatism. Don't try to control everything . . . (be) like a clear mirror which reflects everything. . . . What does the mirror do? It reflects without judgment. And you—you should do likewise. . . . This is the Law or Way of No Truth (i.e., no dogmatic attitude about what you believe to be the Truth.) (Ch 1:1-31)[18]

We recognize Jesus' admonition to avoid coveting things that will decay, to never make a public display of praying and to find a way to be reconciled with our opponents. The Sutras reflect his creative reformulation of them in the delightful imagery of Taoist and Buddhist thought. The Second Law, the Way of No Action, is the Taoist rule of Wu-wei—literally, no action. A correct understanding of this "Golden Rule" of Taoism is that we are to do nothing artificial or unnatural. The idea of polishing the mind, like a mirror, to clean it of dust (ignorance), so that it reflects true reality is a Buddhist metaphor. Chapter Six concludes this Sutra with the words of Ye Su, "Anyone, even if he has only a little love, can walk the Bright Path, and he will suffer no harm. This is the way (Tao) that leads to Peace and Happiness . . . and of Returning to Our True Original Nature." (Ch. 6:13, 14, 25).[19]

The Fourth Liturgica Sutra: The Supreme, Palmer explains, is a beautiful Chinese interpretation of the classic hymn "Gloria in Excelsis." It represents eighth century Christian theology and because it goes beyond the teaching of Ye Su, we will not include it here. This is a good example of how much later redaction was added to what we believe are genuine sayings of Jesus.

The last Sutra that we will study Palmer calls the *Stone Sutra* because, unlike the others, this "manuscript" is written on the twelve-foot high stone stele that Palmer tells us inspired him to search for and retranslate the parchment Sutras. The Stone Sutra contains much of the material that we have already studied, and we need not repeat it. There is, however, a striking visual symbol that dramatically proclaims that Jesus was a pioneer of interfaith dialogue. We first note that this stele is mounted on a huge tortoise because the ancient Chinese believed that the world is supported on the back of a giant turtle. Then, looking up, we see a tablet supported by two dragons. At the top of this tablet is a cross, rising up from a lotus blossom surrounded by clouds and topped by a flaming pearl. The Buddhist lotus represents the beauty of spirituality rising out of the muddy waters of samara (everyday life). The surrounding cloud represent the Yin or passive quality of Nature in Taoist thought and the flaming pearl atop the Cross is the Taoist Yang principle of force in Nature. This impressive symbol beautifully combines the essential ideas of three religions: Taoist Nature mysticism, Buddhist self control and compassion, and Jesus' way of ethical and sacrificial love. Here is empirical evidence that conventional Western Christianity has seriously undervalued the contribution that the real, historical Jesus made to, not one, but at least three developing world religions: Taoism, Buddhism, and

Christianity. Of critical interest for us today is the way the essential spirits of these three faiths have been so beautifully integrated.

I believe that we can now reasonably claim that Jesus (Issa, Bodhisattva, Ye Su) followed the lead of Israel's prophets and dedicated himself to laying the foundation for a new world spirituality. Furthermore, he has provided us with an exciting vision for our new millennium and beyond. It is grounded in the great vision of II Isaiah that inspired Jesus to undertake his post crucifixion, eastern ministry—his final drama.

> It is too light a thing that you
>   should be my servant
>   to raise up the tribes of Jacob
>   and to restore the survivors of
>   Israel.
> I will give you as a light to the
>   nations
>   that my salvation may reach to
>   the end of the earth.
>
> (Isaiah 49:3-6)

But, this is not the end of the drama. It is only the first half. We have learned how Jesus interacted with Brahmanists (Hindus), Buddhists, Zoroastrians, and Taoists and, we believe in some cases made a dramatic and lasting impact. But, he was also influenced by Eastern teachings and upon returning to Palestine incorporated them into his ever expanding gospel. As we turn now to identify some of the material, we will see that much was quite similar to his earlier teachings, but some of it was radically different. So radical for conventional Jewish thinking that it was not readily accepted in the cannon of growing Christian scripture.

Chapter Seven
Jesus: Pioneer of Inter Faith Dialogue

We mentioned earlier that there are elements in the canonical gospels that echo Eastern themes, and we conjectured that this could reflect Essene teachings seeded centuries earlier by King Ashoka's Buddhist missionaries. But our careful study of material recounting Jesus' missionary journey to the East has provided us with enough powerful evidence to claim that Jesus himself learned firsthand about Eastern spirituality. Moreover, we have discovered the reciprocal nature of Jesus' ministry. He was no dogmatic evangelical preacher; always preaching, never listening. Jesus truly loved being with people, and he had learned during his Asian ministry to practice what Thich Nhat Hanh calls "deep listening." This is the basis for his commitment to interfaith dialogue. We will now present material to substantiate this claim by first identifying some Buddhist parallels in the canonical gospels. We begin with Jesus' sayings about the mustard seed of faith. He placed much emphasis on the power of faith to heal and taught his disciples that even a small amount of genuine faith can produce dramatic results. He told them, perhaps using a bit of hyperbole, that if their faith was only mustard seed size, they could move mountains.[1] Let us see how the Buddha used a similar parable about the tiny mustard seed and how even a small amount of faith can change a life.

"And Kisa Gotami had an only son, and he died. In her grief, she carried the dead child to all her neighbors asking them for medicine, and the people said: 'She has lost her senses. The boy is dead. . . .' At length, Kisa Gotami met a man who replied to her . . . 'go to Sakyamuni, the Buddha. . . .' The Buddha answered, 'I want a handful of mustard seeds. . . . The mustard seed must be taken from a house where no one has lost a child, husband, parent, or friend.' Poor Kisa Gotami now went from house to house. . . . (But) there was no house but some beloved one had died in it. . . . And she thought to herself, 'How selfish am I in my grief! Death is common to all; yet in this valley of desolation there is a path that leads to immortality (for one) who has surrendered all selfishness. . . .' Returning to the Buddha, she took refuge in him and found comfort in the Dharma, which is a balm that will sooth all the pains of our troubled hearts."[2] Both stories link life-changing faith with the insignificant little mustard seed. Just a little faith can bring understanding that changes our life.

John records a story about Jesus asking a Samaritan woman for a drink of water. The shocked woman replies, "How is it that you, a Jew, ask a drink of me?" John explains that Jews have nothing to do with the despised Samaritans. Jesus who has no interest in ancient class distinctions, offers her a drink of "living water," saying she will never thirst again. Of course, his language is metaphorical, and he is offering her his Gospel of love which she gratefully accepts.[3]

The Buddhist version as related by Carus is as follows:

> Ananda, the favorite disciple of the Buddha, . . . passed by a well . . . and seeing Pakati, a girl of the Matanga caste, he asked her for water to drink. Pakati said, "O Brahmin, I am too humble and mean to give thee water to drink. . . ." And Ananda replied, "I ask not for caste but for water," and the Matanga girl's heart leaped joyfully, and she gave Ananda to drink. . . . The girl repaired to the Blessed One (Buddha) and cried, ". . . I love Ananda.' And the Blessed One . . ." said, "It is not Ananda that thou lovest, but his kindness. Accept, then, the kindness thou hast seen him practice unto thee, and in the humility of thy station practice it to others."

In both of these stories, life changing love is the theme. Race and caste do not matter. The love that we show begets more love from a well that never will run dry.[4]

Probably the most dramatic of the stories about Jesus is the account of his walking on the water to rejoin his disciples after feeding the multitude. Both Mark and Matthew record this but only Matthew adds the story of Peters' attempt to duplicate this feat.[5] It is clearly a parable about having faith to walk over life's stormy sea and not about literal water walking. This is made obvious when to the sinking Peter, Jesus cries, "O, man of little faith, why did you doubt?" The Buddhist parallel conveys a similar theme.

> When the world-honored Buddha had left Savatthi, Sariputta felt a desire to see the Lord and to hear him preach. Coming to the river where the water was deep and the current strong, he said to himself, "This stream shall not prevent me. I shall go and see the Blessed One," and he stepped upon the water which was as firm under his feet as a slab of granite. When he arrived at a place in the middle of the stream where the waves were high, Sariputta's heart gave way, and he began to sink. But rousing his faith and renewing his mental effort, he proceeded as before and reached the other bank. The people of the village were astonished. . . . And Sariputta replied, "I lived in ignorance until I heard the voice of the Buddha. As I was anxious to hear the doctrine of salvation, I crossed the river, and I walked over its troubled waters because I had faith. . . ." The World-honored One added: "Sariputta, thou hast spoken well. Faith like thine alone can save the world . . . and enable men to walk dry shod and attain deliverance from death."[6]

The story about Jesus healing the man born blind is clearly about spiritual and not physical sight. The healing process is interesting—putting mud on the man's eyes. It appears to be the only account of Jesus using a physical aid and probably reflects an ancient folk healing technique. Whatever the explanation, it clearly would demand that the man have faith in Jesus' power—really God's power working through him—to heal. The point about it being spiritual sight is suggested by the man's and Jesus' comments, "One thing I do know, that though I was blind, now I see." Answering the question as to how he was healed, he says, "Do you also want to become his disciples?" Later, Jesus explains, "I came into this world for judgment so that those who do not see may see, and those who do see may become blind."[7]

Now compare this version with a similar story in the Dhammapada.

> There was a man born blind, and he said, "I do not believe in the world of light and appearance. There are no colors, bright or somber. . . . If colors existed, I should be able to touch them. They have no substance and are not real. Everything real has weight, but I feel no weight where you see color." In those days, there was a physician who was called to see the blind man. He mixed four simples (medicines), and when he applied them to the cataracts of the blind man, the gray film melted, and his eyes acquired the faculty of sight. The Tathagata (Buddha) is the physician, the cataract is the illusion of the thought "I am," and the four simples are the four noble truths.[8]

When we understand that the four noble truths are the Buddha's prescription for healing, we can see the connection with Jesus healing technique. Both stories are about gaining understanding or spiritual insight. In the Johannine account, the man proclaims Jesus to be a prophet presumably because of his ability to channel God's healing love. In the Dammapada story, the man comes to understand and accept Buddha's "medicine," namely that ignorant self-centeredness is the cause of all of our suffering.

Let us next turn to the Taoist tradition and look for similarities in the canonical gospels. Our aim is not to try to identify a perfect match of the sayings of Jesus and Lao Tazu, the author of the *Tao Te Ching*. That is simply not possible because of the language difference and teaching techniques employed by the two masters. What we shall attempt to show is the remarkable congruence of insight and spiritual tone to be found in the two traditions. We begin with Jesus' vision of the universal and all including nature of the coming new world order—the Kingdom of God.

". . . The Kingdom of Heaven is like a net that was thrown into the sea and caught fish of every kind."[9] This same idea of all inclusiveness is found in the *Tao te Ching*. "Heaven's net casts wide. Though its meshes are coarse, nothing slips through."[10]

Jesus often expresses his vision of the coming kingdom with references to nature and trust in its guiding force. "Therefore I tell you, do not worry about your life, what you will eat or what you will drink, or about your body, what you will wear. Is not life more than food, and the body more than clothing? Look at the birds of the air; they neither sow nor reap nor gather into barns, and yet your heavenly father feeds them. Are you not of more value than they? . . . And why do you worry about clothing? Consider the lilies of the field, how they grow; they neither toil nor spin, yet I tell you, even Solomon in all his glory was not clothed like one of these. But if God so clothes the grass of the field . . . will he not much more clothe you—you of little faith?"[11]

The same relaxed trust is an essential part of the teachings of Lao Tzu.

> All things arise from Tao.
> They are nourished by Virtue (faith).
> They are formed from matter.
> They are shaped by environment.
> Therefore all things arise from Tao.
> By Virtue (faith) they are nourished,
> Developed, cared for,
> Sheltered, comforted,
> Grown, and protected. . . .[12]

> Tao abides in non-action (wu wei)
> Yet nothing is left undone.[13]

> The Tao alone nourishes and brings everything to fulfillment.[14]

> The world is ruled by letting things take their course.[15]

Most certainly, Tao can be understood as a non-theistic concept of Ultimate Reality or Ground of All Being. But recall our reading of the *Jesus Sutras* wherein Jesus boldly interprets Tao in terms of a personal, loving God. We are finding similarities in these teachings, but we must not cover up important differences. Jesus respected and was influenced by some insights from other traditions but he remained true to his own deepest spiritual certainties.

Another theme central to Jesus' teaching was that of child-like openness and trust and a genuine humble spirit.

At that time, Jesus said, "'I thank you, Father, Lord of Heaven and earth, because you have hidden these things from the wise and the intelligent and have revealed them to infants. . . .'[16] At that time the disciples came to Jesus and asked, 'Who is the greatest in the Kingdom of Heaven?' He called a child, whom he put among them, and said, 'Truly I tell you, unless you change and become like children, you will never enter the Kingdom of Heaven. Whoever becomes humble like this child is the greatest in the Kingdom of Heaven.[17] The greatest among you will be your servant. All who exhalt themselves will be humbled, and all who humble themselves will be exhalted.'"[18] Jesus did not exempt himself from his teaching about humility. In a striking statement he asks, "Why do you call me good? No one is good but God alone."[19]

Comparison with the *Tao to Ching* reveals several examples of the same spirit.

> Can you be as a new born babe?
> Washing and cleaning the primal vision?
> Can you be without stain? . . .
> Leading yet not dominating,
> This is the Primal Virtue.[20]

> Know the strength of man,
> But keep a women's care!
> Be the stream of the universe,
> Ever true and unswerving,
> Become as a little child once more.[21]

> The sage is shy and humble—to the world
> he seems confusing (sic confused?)
> Men look to him and listen.
> He behaves like a little child.[22]

> Surrender yourself humbly: Then you can be trusted
> to care for all things.
> Love the world as your own self; then you can
> truly care for all things.[23]

One of the central tenants of Jesus' teaching that he shared with the great prophets of Judaism was that of non-violence. We need to be frequently re minded of Jesus' way of non-violent conflict resolution. A clear example of this occurred when one who was with Jesus attempted to defend his master with his sword. "then, Jesus said to him, 'Put your sword back into its place; for all who take the sword will perish by the sword.'"[24]

We find several examples of this same anti-violence sentiment in Lao Tzu's teachings.

> Whenever you advise a ruler in the way of the Tao,
> counsel him not to use force to conquer the universe.
> For this would only cause resistance.
> Thorn bushes spring up wherever the army has passed.
> Just do what needs to be done.
> Never take advantage of power. . . .

> Achieve results,
> But not through violence.
> Force is followed by loss of strength.
> This is not the way of Tao.
> That which goes against the Tao
> Comes to an early end.[25]

Good weapons are instruments of fear; all creatures hate them.
Therefore followers of the Tao never use them.[26]

What others teach, I also teach; that is:
'A violent man will die a violent death!'
This will be the essence of my teaching.[27]

A great country is like low land.
It is the meeting ground of the universe,
the mother of the universe.
The female overcomes the male with stillness,
lying low in stillness. . . .
It is fitting for a great nation to yield.[28]

We will now focus our attention on spiritual insights that seem to reflect an influence from Brahmanism and may account for the mysticism so characteristic of the Fourth Gospel. But before identifying specific material, I would like to call the reader's attention to certain unique features of this gospel that seem to bear directly on our thesis.

Biblical scholars have for long commented on how very different the Fourth gospel is from the first three Synoptic gospels. Indeed, the term "synoptic" means that generally Matthew, Mark, and Luke "see" the Jesus story the same way or "together." The Fourth Gospel stands alone in style, content, and presentation. While some features in the synoptics are present, many are missing. Foot washing replaces the bread and wine sacrament during the final dinner, and Jesus', sayings and parables are replaced with philosophical discourses. Words like light and truth replace stories about the Kingdom of God. Jesus' ministry begins with the temple cleansing drama and continues for three years instead of the one year or eighteen months ministry in the synoptics that place the temple cleansing near the end of the ministry. In one instance Jesus is identified as being "not yet fifty years old," or almost fifty years old, while the synoptics present Jesus as a young man in his early thirties.

It almost seems as if the author were speaking of another Jesus in a quite different ministry. Well, in a way, I believe that is true. The author knew that after recovering from the injuries inflicted on the "Suffering Servant," Jesus had embarked on a extended Asian missionary journey with his twin brother Thomas. He returned, an older man, and began a second Palestinian ministry that included the mystical spirituality so beautifully presented only in the Fourth gospel. By placing the temple cleansing earlier, the author had created space for including material from Jesus' Asian ministry. The temple episode did indeed occur near the end of the first ministry but what follows includes details of a second post Asian Palestinian ministry. The placement of the Passion Story at the end of this gospel could not have been the original author's intention since, in fact, it occurred between the two ministries. But, there is evidence of much redaction in all of the gospels, and especially in the case of the Fourth Gospel, there would have been good reason for it. Paul's version of the Christ story would be flourishing at the time the final redaction of the Fourth gospel was written, c.a. 90-115 C.E., and we know that this was a very controversial gospel and almost did not make it into the cannon of Christian literature. In the light of our thesis, it is not difficult to understand why. I am convinced that the Fourth gospel bears very strong witness in support of our thesis of a post crucifixion ministry.

I have come to believe that one of the most important results of this project is a new hermeneutic for reading the Fourth Gospel. We have noted that New Testament scholars have long recognized how greatly this Fourth Gospel differs from the three synoptic Gospels. My first teacher, Dr. Milo Connick, taught us that the language in this gospel does not contain the literal words of Jesus. A first century Palestinian peasant simply would not speak like that. The language attributed to Jesus is far too sophisticated and the mystic theology is not consistent with the Jewish monotheism in the synoptic gospels. Dr. Connick compared the outline and form of this gospel with a Greek drama. It consists of seven "signs" (miracles) and seven "I Am" sayings that signify to the audience that a divine being is speaking. Later, in seminary at Boston University, Dr. Harold DeWolf suggested that we read the sayings in the third person as *He* is the way, truth, life, and light of the world. Jesus would not have used the dramatic "I am" language to refer to himself, and most certainly, he would never have claimed to be one with his Father-God. Nor would he have said to Philip: "He who has seen me has seen the Father." (John 14:9) Jesus would never have claimed divinity. Why, he even admonished a young man who called him "good," with the remark that only God is good. I followed this line of liberal exegesis for many years, much to the unease of my conservative and fundamentalist students. But my belief that Jesus survived the crucifixion and embarked on a missionary journey to Asia has led me to believe that the controversial language in the Fourth Gospel really must be attributed to Jesus.

The account of Jesus' stay in India is most informative. We have noted the testimony that Jesus, or Issa as he was called there, studied Hindu scriptures with the Brahmin priests, and I believe that the theology of the Upanishads impressed him greatly. Upon his return he shared his new spiritual insights with his "beloved disciple" whom he had asked to wait for his return (21:20-23). The first example of Indian influence can be found in the magnificent prologue to this gospel. In the Greek text, the "Word" is Logos that in Stoic thought is the Creative Wisdom of God that creates the world. But suppose we substitute Sanskrit for the Greek and read:

> In the beginning was the Atman (Cosmic Person) and the Atman was with Brahman (God), and the Atman was Brahman. All things came into being through him, and without him not one thing came into being. What has come into being in him was life and the life was the light of all people. . . . The true light which enlightens everyone. . . .[29]

If we look for a probable source for this version of Creation as presented in the Prologue, there is no better one than the Aitareya Upanishad.

> Before Creation, all that existed was the Self, the Self alone. (In the Mandukya Upanishad, the Self is called the Cosmic Person or Atman.) Nothing else was. Then the Self thought: "Let me send forth the worlds." . . . .
>
> He thought: "Behold the worlds, let me now send forth their guardians." (The persons who dwell on the worlds.) . . . .
>
> He thought: "How shall there be guardians and I have no part in them?" . . . .
>
> He thought: "Let me enter the guardians". . . . Having entered the guardians, he identified himself with them. He became many individual beings.[30]

This Upanishad parallels the thought in the Prologue that proclaims that the Atman or Cosmic Person (Father) is "the true light which enlightens everyone. . . ." In the course of teaching Eastern religious philosophy, I would outline the discipline of Yoga and the successful yogi's final exclamation: "Aham Brahm asmi!," literally "I am Brahman! (God)" or "I have come to recognize my intimate relationship with Brahma-God." This would be followed with "Tat twam assi" or "That thou art" or "and you also are related to the Divine One!" This expresses the Indian monistic belief that Brahman is all that is real, that is, Brahman is the entire universe, including all persons. Because Atman is the Cosmic Soul of Brahman, it would be more accurate to say that Brahma-Atman is the Soul of all that is.[31] The physical space-time universe is really only a "virtual" cosmos, that is, a mental projection from the Mind of God. It is only maya or "illusion." Compare Maya with our words "magic" and "myth."

Many refer to this Hindu concept as pantheism because God is in everything. But Brahmins reject this because it limits the Absolute to what we presently perceive as the "world" whereas, in reality Brahman is much more, being the infinite potential of all that has been and will or could be.

In any event, Jesus must have grasped the point that the concept was perfectly compatible with his own mystical experience of his Father's intimate and continuing presence. Of course, he could say "I and the Father are one and pray that . . . they may all be one. As you Father, are in me and I am in you, may they also be in us." (17:20). "Do you not believe that I am in the Father and the Father is in me?" (14:10) But I do not believe that he could have used this language before learning it from the Upanishads.

Moreover, the "I Am" sayings in the gospel fit perfectly with the language of the Upanishads and the Gita. My colleague, Professor Lal Goel helped me find Sanskrit parallels for some of them. In 8:12, we read: "Again Jesus spoke to them saying, 'I am the light of the world.'" In Sanskrit, this would be "Aham

Chita." Aham meaning "I am" and Chitta being the word for mind or light. In 14:6, we read, "I am the way and the truth and the life." In Sanskrit:, this would be "Aham Yoga" (Way) and "Aham Sattya" (truth) and "Aham Jiva" (life). Professor Goel affirmed that not only rishis (accomplished teachers) but any yogi could quite freely use this language to proclaim their experience of mystical union with Brahma-God.

I found striking parallels to these "I am" sayings while reading in the Bhagavad-Gita, the part where the Lord Krishna (Avatar or Incarnation of the Vishnu mode of Brahman) discloses his divine nature to the great warrior Arjuna. (The Bhagavad-Gita, the Ninth Teaching vv 19-42).

> Listen Arjuna, as I recount
> > for you in essence
> > the divine powers of my self;
> > endless is my extent.
> I am the self abiding
> > in the heart of all creatures; . . . .
> I am Vishnu striding among sun gods. . . .
> I am lightning among wind gods. . . .
> I am the song in sacred love;
> I am Indra, king of the gods;
> I am the mind of the senses,
> > the consciousness of creatures.
> I am gracious Shiva among howling storm gods,
> I am the beginning, the middle, and the end of creations, Arjuna;
> Of sciences, I am the science of the self; . . ,
> I am indestructible time,
> The creator facing everywhere at once.
> Arguna, I am the seed of all creatures;
> Nothing animate or inanimate
> > could exist without me.

Clearly, the "I am" (Aham asmi) formula fits neatly with the "I am" sayings of Jesus in the Fourth Gospel, and I believe Jesus found this style acceptable particularly since it echoed the ancient Hebrew name of God–"Yahweh" or "I am"–the unspoken sacred tetragrammaton. Of course, the polytheistic elements in the Gita; "I am Indra, King of the gods" and "I am Vishnu striding among sun gods" must have been rejected by Jesus. He would have found the language of the monistic Upanishads much more acceptable. It is the view of many scholars of Indian philosophy that the Bagavad-Gita is an attempt to synthesize the polytheism of the ancient Vedas with the monism of the Upanishads that are the latter portion of the Vedic literature.

We need to make a very important distinction now between Jewish theism and the ultimate expression of Indian monism found in Shankara's Advaita Vedanta. As we noted earlier, theists have rejected eastern monism or pantheism because to identify God so completely with the world of nature and finite persons would mean that all the imperfections of nature such as the various forms

of so-called natural evil that range from disasters to diseases and all the ignorance and evil will of humans must be included in the divine nature. But if this is
the weakness of pantheism, its strength is that God being immanent in everything need not break into the world with miracles that would violate His natural
laws. Process theologians suggest that their concept of pan-en-theism allows for
God's intimate relationship with the world of persons and things, thus avoiding
the problem of miracles, but asserts that God remain separate from that which is
imperfect and evil. Intimately related to, but not identical with, is the formula. I
believe that Jesus understood this concept and that allowed him to honestly proclaim his union with God in religious spirit and ethical purpose without the arrogant presumption of being Deity. Indeed, he frequently insists on the Father's
superiority and the Son's dependence on the Father's will.

> "Jesus said to them, 'Very truly, I tell you, the Son can do nothing on
> his own, but only what he sees the Father doing; for whatever the Fa-
> ther does, the Son does likewise.'"
> (5:19)
>
> "I can do nothing on my own. . . . I seek to do not my own will but
> the will of him who sent me."
> (5:30)
>
> "My teaching is not mine but his who sent me."
> (7:16)
>
> "Then Jesus cried aloud: 'Whoever believes in me believes not in me
> but in him who sent me."
> (12:44)
>
> ". . . for I have not spoken on my own, but the Father who sent me
> has himself given me a commandment about what to say and what to
> speak."
> 12:49)
>
> ". . . I am going to the Father, because the Father is greater than I."
> (14:28)

This language convinces me that Jesus is speaking of ethical rather than
metaphysical monism. He experienced oneness with his Father in religious spirit
and ethical purpose while all the while quite aware of God's ontological indi-
viduality and superiority. No Jewish theist would ever claim to be Deity. To be
God inspired—completely and consistently—is quite enough!

Some of the clearest expressions of this kind of mysticism are in the Farewell Discourses and Jesus' Great Prayer. In a discussion with his disciples, Jesus
proclaims: "Believe me that I am in the Father and the Father is in me. . . ."[32]
Later in prayer to his Father-God, he speaks: "I ask not only on the behalf of
these (his disciples who are present), but also on behalf of those who will be-

lieve in me through their word that they all may be one. As you, Father, are in me and I am in you, may they also be in us . . . so that they may be one as we are one. . . ."[33] This mystical language is quite unlike that in the synoptic gospels and very clearly reflects that of Indian Brahmanism. Here is another clear example of how Jesus was open to new ways of understanding God's presence in the world. Jesus had discovered the spiritual monism of the Upanishads. Brahman is in all things and persons. We all share the cosmic Atman Soul that lights up every one of us.

We have noted the close correspondence between the Prologue, the "I am" sayings, the Farewell Discourses, and the Final Prayer of Jesus to his disciples with the Gita and the Aitereya Upanishad. All we needed to do was to substitute Jesus' Jewish vocabulary for the Indian Sanskrit words. On the basis of the data presented, we can argue that the mystical language does indeed come from Jesus. But, it is Jesus Issa who has been traveling, studying, and learning for at least a decade about the metaphysical concepts in India's ancient Upanishads. The "Jesus of history" had become the "Christ of faith." The reader must have noted that I have omitted using John's name in referring to the Fourth Gospel. I will now explain my reasons for doing this.

Rudolph Bultmann and other scholars of the Fourth Gospel, including most recently the Jesus Seminar Group, have found evidence of several literary layers, e.g., the Prologue, the Seven Signs, the I AM material, etc. Moreover, there appears to have been much redacting throughout this Gospel. Conventional scholarship places the date of composition early in the second century C.E., but I believe there is evidence that the earliest formulation was much earlier. Certain passages seem to reflect the reporting of an eyewitness.[34]

I suggest that Chapter 21 refers to the departure of Jesus for his Asian ministry and not his preparation for Ascension into Heaven to be with his Father, as is commonly supposed. Jesus and his friends are walking and. . . .

> Peter turns and saw following them the disciple whom Jesus loved, who had lain close to his breast at the supper and had said, "Lord who is going to betray you?" When Peter saw him, he said to Jesus, "Lord, what about this man?" Jesus said to him, "If it is my will that he remains until I come, what is that to you?"

Who is this mysterious disciple whom Jesus loved? We find a clue in both the Gospel of Mary Magdalene and the Gospel of Philip. Both reveal the special relationship between Mary and Jesus. Philip's Gospel characterizes it as very intimate and tells of Jesus often kissing Mary on her mouth. We can reasonably conclude that Mary was the disciple whom Jesus loved. Moreover, current interest in DaVinci's painting of the Last Supper leads some to conclude that the beardless person sitting at Jesus' right hand is a young woman. This matches the passage quoted above that identifies the person close to Jesus at the Supper as the disciple whom Jesus loved. And if this is the same person referred to in the Mary and Philip Gospels, there can be no question that Mary Magdalene is that disciple. The male words "him," "man," and "he" in the passage clearly are late glosses inserted by a redactor to support the erroneous tradition that the disciple was John, young and beardless, who reclined on Jesus at the Supper. The concluding colophon leads us to a striking conclusion. The author declares, "This is the disciple who is bearing witness to these things and *who has written these things*" (v. 24a). Since this remark immediately follows the passages about the beloved disciple that we identified as Mary Magdalene, *it can only refer to Mary, who clearly identified herself as the author*. Without distortion, we can read the passage as: "I am the disciple who . . . has written these things." Contrary to the two thousand years of false tradition, there seems to me no reasonable way to refute this conclusion. Mary Magdalene was the author of the earliest version of the Fourth Gospel.

Here is a suggested rearrangement of the Fourth Gospel to show how Mary Magdalene might have written her early draft. It has two parts. The first presents a summary of Jesus' first ministry that begins in Judea with Jesus as a disciple of John the Baptizer continues in Sumaria and climaxes with the Crucifixion Drama. The second part summarizes Jesus' later ministry and contains material that Jesus learned during his missionary journeys in Asia. Examples previously noted are repeated to show how Mary integrates them in her gospel. Before we present our outline, we need to note and explain the inclusion of material traditionally identified as the "Seven Signs" and the "Seven I Am Sayings." The "Signs" replace what in the synoptics are called miracles and serve to identify Jesus as the divine Christ. Both the Signs and Sayings are grouped in sevens, perhaps reflecting how seven echoes the Creation Story where God created the world in six days and rested on the seventh, the Sabbath, the holy day in a seven day week. It would appear that a late Redactor, in combining the two parts of Mary's story, has rearranged the numerical sequence of the signs. The original two-part presentation had to be revised by the "Christian" Redactor to preserve the fiction of one ministry culminating in Crucifixion and Resurrection.

Part One: Jesus' First Ministry in Palestine

1:35-45–Jesus, a disciple of John in Judea meets Peter, Andrew, Philip, and Nathaneal.

3:22-26–Jesus argues with John. Baptism with the Holy Spirit (fire) supersedes water baptism and inward purification is more important than cleansing only the outside.

4:1-3–Jesus and his friends flee to Galilee.

2:1-11–The wedding of Jesus and Mary Magdalene.[35] Since both Jesus and Mary are reputed to be of royal blood (Jesus from David and Mary from Benjamin), there is the suggestion of a royal, spiritual leadership for the dawning Kingdom of God. Jesus turns water into wine (the 1st Sign). The wine of Jesus' Way is superior to the Water of ritualistic Judaism.

4:46-54–Jesus heals the Roman official's son. Salvation is offered to everyone (the 2nd Sign).

5:1-17–Jesus heals the Lame Man at the Pool doing the work of his Father even on the Sabbath (the 3rd Sign).

6:1-16–Jesus feeds the Multitudes, a miracle of Sharing Love, that may have included Zealot fighters who try to make him their Leader and King. He is not interested in setting up a political Kingdom nor will he employ the way of violence (the 4th Sign).

11:1-44–Jesus brings Lazarus back to life. Death is not final. God will resurrect all faithful souls to be with Him in Heaven. As we earlier noted, in the Gospel of "Secret Mark," it appears to be a ritual resurrection. It is the 5th Sign in our reconstruction, and the 7th Sign in the conventional ordering.

12:12-15–Jesus rides into Jerusalem on a donkey symbolizing his rejection of violence and the false military, Davidic Messianic Hope. The cheering crowd fails to understand and Jesus weeps over Jerusalem. (c.f. Luke 19:41-44)

2:13-17–Jesus chases the greedy money changers out of the Temple. It should be a sacred place for worship and not a noisy market place.

12:1-8 Mary Magdalene anoints Jesus in preparation for his dangerous ceremonial death role as Israel in the Suffering Servant Drama.

13:3-9, 21-26, 34, 35–The Last Supper before the Drama begins. There is no bread and wine covenant, Jesus washes his disciples' feet, and chooses Judas to play the role of Betrayer. He gives the New Commandment: "Love one another as I have loved you."

18:1-3–Jesus and his disciples go to the Garden of Gethsemane where Judas leads Roman soldiers to arrest Jesus.

18:12-40–Jesus is taken first to Caiaphas to face a charge of blasphemy, then to Pilate to face political charges that he refuses to pay taxes to Rome, and he claims to be King of the Jews (Israel). Jesus replies: "My Kingdom is not of this world." Pilate offers to release Jesus and punish Zealot Barabbas in his stead. The mob refuses and cries out that in pretending to be a King, Jesus has challenged Caesar. Pilate, fearful of Roman reprisal, condemns Jesus to be crucified as "King of the Jews." (c.f. Mark 14:52-65 and Luke 23:1, 2)

19:25-37–Jesus' Mother, her sister, and Mary Magdalene are present. When Jesus sees Mary, "the disciple whom he loved," he says to his Mother, "Behold your daughter," (the word "son" is a later redaction to preserve the fiction that it was John), and to Mary, "Behold your Mother" (vv. 25-27). Jesus cries out, "I thirst" and drinks a prepared soporific drug (not vinegar), that he may appear to be dead. He says: "It is finished," meaning that the first part of the Drama of Suffering Israel is over, then he loses consciousness (vv. 28-30). A soldier ceremoniously pierces his side with his spear but does not break his legs, probably by a prearranged bribe by Joseph of Arimathea.

19:38-42–Joseph of Arimathea and Nicodemus carry Jesus' body to a private tomb. Pilate granted Joseph Jesus' body probably because he had been bribed. Nicodemus has brought a supply of medical herbs.

20:1-20–Mary Magdalene comes to the tomb and sees that the covering stone has been rolled back. She ("the one whom Jesus loved") tells Peter and both return to the tomb to find that Jesus' body is not there. Mary sees two "angels" in white clothing (this is the traditional garment of the Essenes who were noted for their healing powers). Mary weeps and explains to another person she believes to be the gardener, that she cannot find Jesus' body. It is in fact, Jesus in disguise, whom Mary recognizes as soon as he speaks her name. She rushes to embrace him but he stops her, probably because he is feeling much bodily pain. He promises to see all of them soon and Mary rushes to tell the disciples that she has seen Jesus alive! Later, Jesus joins his friends and to prove that it is really he, shows them his wounded hands and side.

20:24-29–Thomas cannot believe, but is convinced when Jesus later sees him. Thomas is overjoyed: the Drama of Israel's Rescue has been played out at a cost of much suffering for Suffering Servant Jesus.

21:1-12–Later, the disciples go fishing and Mary recognizes Jesus building a fire on the beach. He invites them to bring their fish and have breakfast with him.

13:36–Peter then asks the departing Jesus, "Where are you going?" Jesus answers, "Where I am going you cannot follow me now."

14:28a–"I go away and (but) I will come (return) to you."

16:19–"A little while and you will see me no more; again a little while and you will see me."

21:20-23–Peter sees "the disciple whom Jesus loved" following them and asks, "What about her!" (We use the correct female pronoun) Jesus responds that he has asked her to wait (and assume leadership?) until he returns. The sharp words "and that is not your concern" reflects Jesus' annoyance at Peter's hostile and jealous feelings toward Mary that is so clearly revealed in the Gospel of Mary. This would be clearly understood if Jesus had indeed appointed Mary, instead of Peter, to lead in teaching the "Jesus Way."

7:34-36–Jesus says, "You will seek me and not find me." They wondered if he was going "to the Dispersion among the Greeks and teach the Greeks." Jesus only says, "Where I am going you cannot come."

This is the end of Mary's account of Jesus' early ministry in Palestine. We need not here include his intervening Ministry in Asia, as we have presented evidence for it in earlier chapters. Now we will present the rest of Mary's Gospel, summarizing the new teaching of Jesus that reflects his commitment to interfaith dialogue.

Part Two: The Mystical Teachings of Jesus

1:1-5–The Logos Prologue: "In the beginning was the Word." In the Greek it is: "In the beginning was the 'Logos'"—the divine power that creates cosmos through speech. Mary's powerful poem recalls the Genesis Creation story where God creates through speech: and God said, "Let there be Light and there was Light!" As we have earlier noted, Mary's creation poem also closely resembles the language and ideas of the Aitareya Upanishad: "In the beginning was the Atman," that is, the Self or Cosmic Soul of Brahman-God. In both traditions, God and Brahman create the cosmos and all that is in it, including finite souls, and then enters the universe to dwell within all beings.

8:57a–Jesus is said to be "not yet fifty years old" and that is quite a bit older than the younger Jesus in his thirties who departed for India. Almost fifteen years have passed and an older, more learned and mature Jesus now uses language that reflect his new understanding of his relationship of his Father-God that is available to every person. As the tradition develops, Jesus is included in the Buddhist stories that he has learned.

4:7-24–Jesus offers the Woman at the Well: "living water" this parallels a previously noted Buddhist story about growing in faith and understanding.

6:16-20–Jesus walks on the water. This story of "water walking" by faith also parallels a Buddhist one (the 6th Sign).

9:1-4–Jesus cures the Man Born Blind with medicinal clay. This curing of "spiritual blindness" is also paralleled in Buddhist literature (the 7th Sign).

Mary's account of Jesus' later teachings now turns from ideas gained from Buddhism to insights and language derived from his study with the Indian Brahmins. We have earlier noted the similarity of the Seven "I am" sayings with some of Lord Krishna's saying in the Bhagavad Gita. They reflect Jesus' certainty that he is the instrument of God called to reveal his Father's will for a new Way of Living with God's healing and energizing love.

6:35	I am the Bread of Life.
8:12	I am the Light of the World.
10:7-9	I am the Door (to Salvation).
10:14	I am the Good Shepard.
11:25	I am the Resurrection and the Life.
14:6	I am the Way and the Truth and the Life. No one comes to the Father, but by me.
15:1-5a	I am the True Vine . . . and you are branches. . . . Love one another as I have loved you.

Mary's summary of Jesus' new teaching concludes with the mystical passages that are traditionally called the "Farewell Discourses" and the "Great Prayer" supposedly offered to his disciples just prior to his arrest and crucifixion to make the story support the emerging Pauline theology. The idea that Jesus had traveled to India and learned profound religious truths from a non-Semitic religion would not have been acceptable.

10:30–Jesus declares: "I and the Father are One!" As we earlier noted, this parallels the Yogi's declaration: "*Aham Braham Asmi*"–"I am Brahman."

5:30–"The Son only does the will of the Father." Jesus frequently asserts that the Son is subordinate to the Father. Jesus believes that his will has become "one" with the Will of his Father—not that he is God the Father!

17:3–"Eternal Life is to know God and his Christ (the Son)." It can begin *now*, (realized eschatology), and not in the future (apocalyptic eschatology).

17:11b, 20-22–Jesus prays that his disciples—and all persons—may be "One", even as he and the Father are One. This parallels the Yogi's declaration: "*Tat Tuam Assi,*" "That thou Art," or and you are also one with Brahman.

21:24-25–We have earlier discussed the ending of this gospel noting that the "beloved disciple," Mary Magdalene declares herself to be the author. She has not included the earlier teachings of Jesus recorded in "Q" or the Sayings Gospel. Mary did not need to replicate that which had been in circulation and was well known by the Jesus people. During her own ministry, she would have had access to "Q" and may even have contributed to its formation.

The great theological insights of Jesus, recorded by Mary, would seem very strange and even offensive to people from the Semitic theistic tradition. Pauline Christians would be terribly confused and Paul was enraged to hear reports of a "new gospel" (Gal. 1:6-9). Even after redaction—perhaps several—the so-called Fourth Gospel had a stormy history because of the radical teachings and almost did not make it into the canon of Scriptures that comprise the orthodox Christian Bible. The contrived tradition that John, one of the original disciples of Jesus, had composed his theological reflections in his old age served to assuage their misgivings and allow it to be accepted as the Gospel of John.

My conclusion is that it is really the Gospel of Mary. Moreover, it is not the Fourth and last to be written Gospel but, in fact, the First Gospel.[36] I refer not to the Gospel as it has been edited and is part of the accepted New Testament. The consensus of scholars is that the final version was probably composed early in the second century. My conclusion is based on my reconstruction that I believe is the earliest version of the Gospel, written by Mary. She used Jesus' own language to record stories learned from conversations with Buddhists, Brahmanists and, most important, his own mystical experiences and mature theology. I submit this as another specific example of the claim that Jesus was a pioneer of interfaith dialogue and prophet of world spirituality.

Of course we cannot speak about Jesus' relationship with Islam because that religion did not come into being in a formal sense until the sixth century C.E. I say "formal sense" because Muslim's believe that any one who confesses belief in the one and only God (by whatever name) and accepts the teachings proclaimed by Muhammad the prophet is, irrespective of time, a Muslim. By their reckoning, Jesus was a Muslim as were all the prophets before him. Even so, there are references to Jesus to be found in the Qur'an including theological comments about his relationship to God and his role as prophet. Recall how at the very beginning of our study we referred to passages in the Qur'an that denied that Jesus died by crucifixion. It is a sad fact that most Christians do not know that Jesus plays an important role in Islam and is very greatly respected and honored by Muslims. Even though I have known and taught this for many years, I was quite surprised to discover Tarif Khalidi's fascinating book *The Muslim Jesus: Saying and Stories in Islamic Literature.*

The reader who knows something about Islam knows that in addition to the Qur'an, recited by Muhammad, there is the *Hadith* or sayings of Muhammad. These fascinating stories focusing on wisdom and piety offer glimpses into the person and mind of the Prophet that are not to be found in the Qur'an. Included is a description of his handsome appearance, his lively sense of humor, and his concern for the welfare of animals.

Students of New Testament scholarship know about "Q" or *Quelle*, the German word for source or sayings of Jesus that we have earlier referred to. But, I had not known that the literature of Islam contained a parallel Hadith, or saying, of Jesus in Arabic. There are several hundred of these sayings and Khalidi has very carefully translated them, and identified the names of the Arabic scholars who recorded them including the dates. The fact that the Arabian Muslim scholars who collected these Hadith of Jesus lived in a time span from the eighth to the eighteenth century C.E. should not diminish our appreciation for their great value. Any student of biblical criticism knows full well that the date of composition of a story need not be, and usually is not, the same date for the event or insight recorded.

Khalidi tell us:

> The Islamic image of Jesus first took shape in the Qur'an, and it is from here that the Muslim gospel of Jesus emanates.

> It is now commonly recognized that Islam was born in a time and place where the figure of Jesus was widely known. From inscriptions, from Syria, Ethiopia, and Byzantine sources, . . . a picture is emerging of a pre-Islamic Arabia where diverse Christian communities, in Arabia itself or in its immediate vicinity, purveyed rich and diverse images of Jesus. It is well to remember that when Islam arrived on the scene of history, the Church of the Great Councils had not yet enforced its dogma in the Near East.[37]

I include these remarks by Khalidi because they justify our including the Hadith of Jesus in our study. Note his remark that the sources for these sayings are from Syria, Byzantine, and Ethiopia—from the East, and not from Palestine. While this does not exclude some early Palestinian traditions, it does strongly argue for a later, post-crucifixion ministry in Asia. It is also germaine that he observes that the Pauline theology of the Christ cult was not widespread in the Near East, even as late as the sixth century C.E.

Let us sample a few of these Hadith of Jesus and see if they might provide us with a window through which we can get yet another understanding of the post-crucifixion ministry of Jesus.

> Jesus was asked, "Spirit and Word of God, who is the most seditious of men?" He replied, "The scholar who is in error. If a scholar errs, a host of people will fall into error because of him."
> Abdallah ibn al-Mubarak (d. 181 A.H./797 A.D. and others)

> 32 . . . They said, "What is the best of worship, Spirit of God?" He said, "Humility before God."
> Ahmad ibn Hanbal (d. 241 A.H./855 A.D. and others)

> 47 . . . Jesus was asked, "How can you walk on water?" He replied, "Through certainty of faith." . . . .
> Ahmad ibn Hanbal (d. 241 A.H./855 A.D. and others)

If we are correct in understanding that this water walking story is originally from Buddhism, it would strengthen our thesis that there was a post crucifixion ministry and this Hadith could be a partial record of it.

49 . . . Jesus used to prepare food for his followers, then call them to eat and wait upon them saying: "This is what you must do for the poor."

Ahmad ibn Hanbal (d. 241 A.H./855 A.D. and others)

51 . . . Jesus said to his disciples, ... "Those among you who sorrow most in misfortune are the most attached to this world."

Ahmad ibn Hanbal (d. 241 A.H./855 A.D. and others)

One would you be hard pressed to find a better example of Buddhist influence.

54 . . . A man who had committed adultery was brought to Jesus. . . . Jesus said, "But no one should stone him who has committed what he has committed." They let the stones fall from their hands. . . .

Ahmad ibn Hanbal (d. 241 A.H./855 A.D. and others)

This is almost an exact parallel to the gospel story except that it is a *man* who has been caught! Does this not provide us with a glimpse into Jesus' non-sexist ethos?

66 . . . Jesus was walking . . . with one of his disciples. A man crossed their path and prevented them from proceeding, saying, "I will not let you pass until I have struck each of you a blow." . . . . Jesus said, "Here is my check. Slap it." The man slapped it and let him pass. He then said to the disciple, "I will not let you pass until I have slapped you too." The disciple refused. When Jesus saw this, he offer him the other check. He slapped it and allowed both to go.

Ahmad ibn Hanbal (d. 241 A.H./855 A.D. and others)

This is similar to the gospel teaching about turning the other check except that in this tradition, accepting the slap has vicarious power that serves another. The disciple benefits from the indignity intended for him but borne by Jesus. It almost hints at the Suffering Servant theme in Isaiah. 53.

81 . . . Jesus was seen leaving the house of a prostitute. Someone said to him, "Spirit of God, what are you doing in the house of this woman?" "It is the sick that a physician visits," he replied.

Abu`Uthman al Jahiz (d. 255 A.H./868 A.D. and others)

88 . . . Jesus was asked, "Which of your deeds is the best? He answered, "Leaving alone that which does not concern me."

Abu`Uthman al Jahiz (d. 255 A.H./868 A.D. and others)

This saying could reflect the Taoist teaching of *wu wei* or letting alone adding support to the idea of a post Palestinian ministry in China.

> 98 . . . "Blessed is he who sees with his heart but whose heart is not in what he sees."
>
>   'Abdallah ibn Qutaba (d. 271 A.H./884 A.D. and others)

Khalidi sees no gospel parallel, but I believe it is a corollary to "Blessed are the pure in heart for they shall see God."

> 103 . . . Jesus passed by a cow which was calving in great distress. "O word of God," the cow said, "pray that God will deliver me." Jesus prayed, "O Creator of the soul from the soul, begetter of the soul from the soul, deliver her." The cow dropped its young.
>
>   Abdallah ibn Qutayba (d. 271 A.H./884 A.D. and others)

Several of these Arabic sayings are about Jesus relating to animals in a manner that reveals Jesus' compassion for them. The language suggests the Indian belief that all souls (atman or jiva) come from the cosmic Atman. All beings, human and animal are precious because they proceed from and remain related to God. The Buddhist idea of compassion for all sentient beings is also relevant. Here is more evidence to support the claim that Jesus had an Eastern ministry.

> 128 . . . A pig passed by Jesus. Jesus said, "Pass in peace." He was asked, "Spirit of god, how can you say this to a pig?" Jesus replied, "I hate to accustom my tongue to evil."
>
>   Abu Bakr ibn Abi al-Dunya (d. 281 A.H./894 A.D. and others)

This is another saying that shows Jesus' respect for all of God's creatures even if religious custom pronounces them unclean. Khalidi includes a very interesting comment from the scholar Ignaz Goldziher who asserts "that the saying is 'undoubtedly' of Buddhist origin."[38]

> 137 . . . Jesus was asked, "Who was your tutor?" "None," he replied. "I saw the ugliness of ignorance and avoided it."
>
>   Ibn 'Abd Rabbihi (d. 328 A.H./940 A.D. and others)

Here is another saying that reflects the Buddhist idea that ignorance is the root of all evil. Because of our ignorance, we believe we have an ego that is the root of selfish carving that results in suffering. It also reflects the Taoist idea of opposites. In this case, ugly ignorance would suggest the goodness of understanding.

> 159 . . . Then he (Jesus) passed by and came upon others who were worshipping and said, "Who are you?" They said, "We are lovers of God! We worship Him not out of fear of hell or longing for paradise, but out of love for Him and to His greater glory." So Jesus said, "You are truly the friends of God, and it is with you that I was commanded to live." And he resided among them.

Abu Talib al-Makki (d. 386 A.H./996 A.D. and others)

Khalidi comments that "Loving God selflessly . . . was a sentiment ascribed to early Sufis. . . ."[39] He also notes that the great Muslim theologian Al-Ghazali (d. 505 A.H./ 1111 A.D.) called Jesus "Prophet of the Heart."[1] I would note that Jesus' statement about his being commanded to *live* reinforces our thesis that God did not send him to *die*.

> 282 . . . Al-'Uris saw in his sleep Christ Jesus Son of Mary . . . (and) .
> . . ask him, "Did the crucifixion really happen?" Jesus said, "Yes, the crucifixion really happened."
> Jamal al-Din ibn Wasil (d. 697 A.H./1298 A.D. and others)

Khalidi says that Al 'Uris was a historical person who was himself crucified. The Qur'an states that Jesus was not killed by crucifixion and the dream referred to the dreamer. In agreement with our argument that the brutal act of crucifixion need not result in death, it is interesting that this hadith affirms that Jesus was crucified but, in accordance with Qu'ranic teaching, did not die.

These saying of Jesus, cherished by Muslims, provide evidence of Jesus' continuing spiritual and ethical growth during his Asian ministry. His new found sensitivity regarding animals is especially interesting. But we must include evidence of the great influence Jesus had on Muhammad whose insights led him to recite the Qur'an six centuries later. Here I am expressing my understanding of revelation as a cooperative phenomenon between God and a sensitive recipient. The brilliant Muhammad had learned much about Arabian polytheism, Judaism, Christianity, and Zoroastrianism during his caravan journeys These insights were funded in his subconscious mind and dramatically released into his consciousness in his encounter with God, mediated by one he called Gabriel.

Specific beliefs about Jesus found in the Qur'an include: the virgin birth tradition, that he was a controversial prophet "embroiled in polemic," to use Khalidi's language[41], the teachings of Jesus in his Gospel or "Evangel" as it is called in the Qur'an and, finally, the belief that Jesus will return at the End Time to pass God's final judgment. Khalidi's summarized Jesus legacy as "gentleness, compassion, and humility."[42] These Arabian sayings of Jesus are parallel in some respect to the "Q" sayings and those in the gospel of Thomas that are not included in the canonical Gospels. Because they are wisdom sayings about proper conduct, ethical values, and piety, a number of contemporary scholars have concluded that Jesus behaved and spoke like a cynic sage.[43] The material that we have included in this chapter is convincing evidence for our theory that Jesus-Issa, Bodhisattva, Je Su, not only influenced Hindu Brahmanists, Buddhists, Taoists, and eventually, Islam but also learned from them and brought back to Palestine parables from Buddhist and Taoist sayings and deep metaphysical insights from the Upanishads. I have expressed my belief that upon his reunion with Mary Magdalene, Jesus shared the stories and insights that had enriched his own ever-growing faith and with Mary's creative writing talent, produced the great Gospel of the Spirit.

If he had returned in the mid 40s or 50s, it would be before the canonical gospels were written and would provide ample time for the parables and metaphysical insights to become part of the oral traditions that would be incorporated into the gospels. Conventional scholarship identifies several components: the sayings of Jesus from "Q" (Quelle is German for source); Mark's account of the acts of Jesus, and Matthew and Luke's use of "special sources" called "M" and "L". I believe that we have supplied evidence for adding the specific material from Brahmanism, Buddhism, and Taoism to those sources. Let us call them the Asian sources or "A". Furthermore, we have good reasons for claiming that it was Jesus, himself, who transmitted this material. Truly, Jesus was an important promoter of interfaith dialogue between Asia and Palestine. It is becoming more and more apparent that there is more literal truth in Mary Magdalene's gospel than we supposed. Considering all the evidence that we have analyzed in the foregoing chapters, we find new meaning in Mary's closing words. "But there are also many other things that Jesus did; if every one of them were written down, I suppose that the world itself could not contain the books that would be written."[44]

Chapter Eight
Prophet of World Spirituality

To answer the question "Why has this tradition been suppressed?," we can suggest two reasonable answers. First, we must remember how furious the Romans would be to learn that the judicial system of their great empire had been frustrated by a small group of Jewish peasants. For a time at least, the followers of Jesus would hide the truth to avoid Roman wraith. Secondly, a new theology and church was being developed by a group called Christians. This developing Christian theology was closely related to ancient mystery religions based on the premise that the fertility god must be sacrificed at harvest time and be resurrected in the spring as part of the eternal cosmic cycle governing all living creatures. Of course, the original followers of the Way—the Jesus people—rejected this concept because it did not fit at all with their Jewish faith or the Jesus traditions they knew.[1] Most of them probably did not know about the well kept secret of Jesus' rescue from the cross, his hurried escape, and his missionary journey to Asia.

It was Paul who skillfully integrated the Jewish Jesus story with the gentile resurrection myth.[2] For him, Jesus was the "Christ." This Greek word originally was substituted for the Hebrew word messiah meaning anointed one but soon came to mean God the Son who had been foreordained by the Father God to assume human form and suffer crucifixion in order that the sins of all believers could be forgiven. His tragic death would be followed, in three days, by his dramatic resurrection and return to heaven but the ascended Lord Jesus' Holy Spirit would always be available to guide the believers in the growing Christian Church. We see here a foreshadowing of the doctrine of the Trinity that would not be formulated for another two centuries. Clearly any announcement that Jesus was still alive and teaching would completely demolish the powerful idea that Jesus, the Lord's anointed, had died for our sins. This would also be true of Paul's formula about eating the body and drinking the blood of Jesus, thereby uniting believers in mystical fashion with their risen Lord. Of course, the story of Jesus' true fate had to be suppressed, and it was, almost completely. But we have seen that in India the story of Jesus' continuing ministry in Asia was preserved.

Supporting my contention that Jesus is prophet of world spirituality, return to the point earlier made about Jesus' desire to share the Jewish idea of one God with the non-theistic Buddhists. This passionate desire to share his monotheism was solidly based on his powerful life changing baptism experience when he had encountered the personal parent-like God who had claimed him as his son. For Jesus, this was not a theological point to be argued, it was a certainty based on direct experience. We have earlier noted at this time, early in the first century, there were still Buddhists in India engaging in serious and sometimes fierce arguments with the Brahmanists who believed that Brahman was the Cosmic Soul inherent in every part of the cosmos. However, the early Theraveda Buddhists were preoccupied with eliminating suffering and so had no time for what to them seemed like abstract metaphysical nonsense. They insisted on following their sense empirical way of Patya Samutpada (Pali), Paticca Samuppada (Sanskrit) meaning codependent origination.[3] This is the concept that all things are enmeshed in an interdependent web of multipliable causes and effects that operates automatically without need of a governing personal deity. But Jesus must have argued with them that their understanding was incomplete. The Buddhist doctrine of universal compassion for all living things was, indeed, true for Jesus. But in his Jewish thinking, their must be an ultimate ground for this karuna love just as his Father God was the ground for hesed and agape love. Even, more certainly, this God must be the compassionate Person who is the ground of all ethical love by whatever name.

The Buddhists would probably have been greatly impressed by Jesus just as he was with their non-violent, compassionate living. Between the sophisticated metaphysical arguments of the Brahmanists and Jesus' witnessing to his own religious experience, fortified by his powerful charismatic personality that probably continued to cure many, some Theravadans must have begun to move beyond atheism. For it is at just about this time that Buddhism begins to mutate into Mahayana; the theistic form of Buddhism. Of course, many a fierce objection has been made to this! Buddhism is not a religion, it is claimed. It is more like a philosophy or, better still, a psychology. This is quite true, I admit, if one is talking about Theravada Buddhism. Two of the philosophical interpretations that had developed this philosophy were the Vaibhashika and Sarvastivada systems of atomic realism that reduced everything to matter/energy.[4]

But if one makes a careful study of Mahayana, particularly in its later stages of development that features the Trikaya trinity, it should become very clear that the Dharmakaya (Kaya = body of the Dharma = Law of all Being) is a first principle just as God the Father is first principle in the Christian Trinity. Furthermore, this first principle of Mahayana, sometimes called "Buddha Mind" must be, at least, personal if it is the Cosmic Buddha that grounds karuna compassion. Now it is true that the great Indian epic, the Mahabehrata (Great War) that includes the Bhagavad Gita (Song of the Lord) was composed at this time and the Gita (for short) must be recognized as theistic. We earlier noted the three modes of the Hindu trinity, the Trimurti or three bodies of Brahman. Vishnu is that feature of Brahman that grounds the Moral Law, sends forth the Lord Krishna, an avatar or descender, who takes on human form and teaches the yogic path to salvation.

One could argue that this Indian theism would be quite enough to account for the emergence of Mahayana, but I believe that our earlier arguments about Jesus' presence in India, and his own very powerful presence in teaching and healing and especially in witnessing to his unshakeable theism should also be factored into this equation. If this is true, as I firmly believe it to be, then Jesus was not only a great Rabbi and Jewish prophet but also, in the best sense of the term, a Bodhisattva (a Buddhist Saint). More accurately, I claim that he was *the* Boddhisatva who was instrumental in guiding the evolution of Buddhism from non-theistic Theravada to theistic Mahayana. In the best sense, Thich Nhat Hanh would be correct in affirming that Sithartha Buddha and Jesus are brothers![5] That Jesus realized the compatibility of his Jewish faith with Buddhism is evidence that Jesus was developing his vision of *world* spirituality.

Jesus' teachings and, most important, his amazing ability to bring us into the divine presence also reached out to the Taoists of China. We discovered in the Jesus Sutras, that Jesus must have been impressed with the Taoists' refreshing childlike belief in the essential goodness of human beings that will enable them to live without violence and, one day, live together in a worldwide community of justice, peace, and love. In Mary's gospel, we saw how Jesus had integrated the mystical metaphysics of Brahmanism into his growing vision of world spirituality. He must have been struck by the compatibility of world religions, when he focused on the highest and best in them. Because of this, Jesus was able to relate to Hindu Brahmanists, Buddhists and Taoists in significant and creative ways.

An honest evaluation compels us to recognize that this does not mean that all of these different ways to God are the same. They are not! We saw clearly in the several manuscripts that Jesus did disagree and argue with the devotes of Brahmanism, Buddhism, and Taoism about social ethics and the divine nature. I believe that we have developed a strong case for believing that Jesus made a significant contribution to the emergence of theistic Buddhism and, perhaps, also in sowing the seeds of compassion he contributed to moderating the caste and sacrifice features of Brahmanism. His own instincts regarding the intrinsic worth of all living beings and, indeed, all of nature were surely reinforced by Buddhist and Taoist spirit of reverence for nature.

We began our study of Jesus' secret ministry by noting that in Palestine his various titles included Rabbi, Messiah, Lord, Savior, and Christ. During his secret ministry, in Asia, Jesus was called Issa or Lord in India, Ye Su, or Righteous Sage, in China and following Thich Nhat Hanh's guidance we suggested that he was regarded as a Bodhisattva in Tibet. Our study enables us to add the new titles: Pioneer of interfaith dialogue and Prophet of world spirituality.

With the passage of time, I believe that appreciation for the influence Jesus had on the spiritual evolution of the various religious cultures will continue to grow. But this story has two sides. It also works the other way around. Each of these different religious cultures also influenced Jesus in very significant ways, and we have noted how he incorporated important insights from them into his Palestinian Gospel. We have an ongoing spiritual dialectic here and the end is not in sight. In the meantime we must continue to do as Jesus did and practice open mindedness toward all religions. This is not a call for ending critical thinking and plunging into blind faith. But, it does mean that the closed minded, dogmatic attitude of fundamentalism can no longer be tolerated. The "only way" formula can be especially dangerous. However, I will suggest a way to save this valuable idea.

Each religion has its core value and its unique way to express it.[6] Christians can rightfully proclaim that Jesus is the only way to know God as the compassionate Mother/ Father God. Buddhists can claim that Gautama Buddha is the only way to complete self-control and mastery of suffering. Brahmanists can claim that Krishna is the only way to understand the relationship between our finite self and our divine Self. Taoists can teach that Lao Tzu is the only way to enter into a mystical relationship with nature. Jews can assert that the prophets are the only way to learn about the Moral Law, and Muslims can say that Muhammad is the only way to integrate piety into everyday living.

Now, of course, there is a caveat to our suggestion regarding the "only way" claims. Almost every religion contains one or more of the several values identified. The point is that each religion emphasizes its core value more than the sister faiths. As long as we are reasonable, there is no reason why the "only way" claims should contradict one another. Hopefully, the time is not far off when we will be able to construct a spiritual mosaic—a multi-religious mandala proclaiming spiritual harmony—without destroying the several religious paths to the One Who is the eternal and omnipresent Ground of All Being in *all* religions. This is the vision that called Jesus to his Asian mission and his daring and successful efforts in working with persons of other faiths should accord him the title Prophet of world spirituality.

Acceptance of the crucifixion survival and Asian ministry theory leads us to ask about the conclusion of Jesus' life. There is an ancient and persistent tradition in France that tells of Mary Magdalene coming to Europe under the care of Joseph of Aramethea. She found refuge in a castle in the Pyrenees in Northern Spain where is enshrined the famous Black Madonna that, according to this tradition, is really Mary Magdalene disguised—hence black. From there, the legend takes her to southern France where she teaches the way of Jesus.

I knew of this tradition but my colleague, Dr. Pierre Kaufke, professor of French language and culture, surprised me when he said that a wider tradition explains that Jesus sent Mary to France to continue teaching about The Way. I have suggested that after returning from Asia he rejoins Mary and together they compose the Spiritual Gospel.

What finally became of Jesus? Laurence Gardner, in *Bloodline of the Holy Grail*, records the tradition that Jesus did go to India with Thomas and then on to Kashmir where he died at Srinagar and was there entombed.[7] Our reconstruction has suggested that Jesus returned to Palestine. The Kashmir burial theory would mean that after a second Palestinian ministry during which he shared his new mystical insights with Mary, Jesus made a last journey to Asia where he died. It is Benjamin who offers the fullest account of this tradition. He agrees that Jesus died in Kashmir and provides photographic evidence of his alleged tomb in Mohalla Khanigar, Srinagar. The tomb is called Rozabal and Benjamin says may scholars have written about it. He describes it as follows:

> At the end of a small triangular park is a timber and brick structure, single storied, with a corrugated sheet roof. One cannot imagine that this modest structure could be preserving the mortal remains of a great prophet whose philosophy and faith have endured for 2000 years.[8]

Benjamin further refers to Professor Fida Hasnain, formerly Director of Archaeology in Kashmir, author of *The Fifth Gospel*, who asserts that in the cellar below the structure is the sepulcher where Jesus' body was entombed.[9]

Michael Baigent, *et al.*, in *Holy Blood, Holy Grail* also recognizes the Kashmir tradition but suggests an alternative theory based on a recent discovery by an Australian journalist he identifies as Joyce, author of *The Jesus Scroll*.[10] The excavation at Masada, that fell to Roman attack in 74 C.E., produced a remarkable scroll; so remarkable that Joyce was asked to smuggle it out of the country. He was fearful of doing this but he did read it. The author of the letter described himself as eighty years old and last of the rightful kings of Israel. It was signed Yeshua ben Ya'akob ben Gennesareth. In English it reads: Jesus of Gennesareth, son of Jacob. Joyce believes that he was none other than Jesus of Nazareth who died in the Roman attack on Masada.

Whichever version of Jesus' final resting place is true, I believe that the data we have presented supports the claim that he made a grand missionary tour from Palestine to India, Kashmir, Tibet, China, and returned to Palestine where he rejoined his wife Mary. After her death, he made a final journey to Kashmir. Here was a missionary journey at least as great as all three of Paul's journeys combined. Clearly if the truth about Jesus' mission were widely known, the theological impact on traditional Christianity would be very great, and as I have argued, promote a positive, revised Christology.

This new Christology would focus on Jesus' vision of God's new world order for planet earth. His revolutionary teachings are the blueprint; though, shamefully, they are represented by only a comma in the Apostle's Creed! We can summarize them from his beatitudes.

Fortunate are those humble, merciful, and gentle people who with pure hearts, work courageously for truth, justice, and world peace. They are the charter members of God's new world community of peace and good will.

The dominant theme of our study is that Jesus did not die by crucifixion. Jesus intended this to be a powerful drama to illustrate how Israel would survive Roman oppression just as he survived crucifixion. Moreover, he intended to renew hope for the future because God would empower Israel to bring about a new kind of society. It was necessary that Jesus live to carry his message of good news to non-Israelites—the people of the East. It was this reciprocal ministry of giving and receiving spiritual truths that we have identified in some detail.

It is time to understand Jesus in a new light. We should no longer say that Jesus died for us as a substitutionary payment for our sins. We have for centuries put too much emphasis on his supposed death in which a loving father-god deliberately sacrificed his only son so that the rest of us could be saved by his blood! This is not only bad theology that gives us an unacceptable model of a loving Father God, it is also ghastly ethics. It was Ezekiel who proclaimed that each individual person is responsible for his own ethical choices. No one can take responsibility for another's moral state. Now is the time to start saying: Jesus lived—better yet, thinking of his loving spirit that is still with us—Jesus *lives* to reveal God's caring, compassionate, personal nature, to show us how to heal one another, to learn non-violent ways of conflict resolution, and how to cooperate with God in incorporating ideas from all the great world religions to build the beloved community (Koinonia) on planet Earth—and, perhaps, beyond.[11] In a manner far surpassing anything the author of the Letter of the Hebrews could have possibly imagined, Jesus was indeed, "The pioneer and perfector of our faith." He acted out with every ounce of his God filled being the two great visions of Second Isaiah. Israel, as God's Suffering Servant will not be extinguished by any disaster and as God's Missionary Servant, will carry God's Gospel of a new world order to all the nations.[12]

Chapter Nine
Afterword

I have been greatly challenged to write this book for two reasons. First, as a member of the community of scholars, I am continually reminded to be very careful and scrupulously honest about collecting, evaluating, and assembling all data. This includes checking, so far as possible, the credentials of the various authors, comments by critical reviewers, and publication data. As a philosopher, I have been taught that in the realm of empirical data, we can never claim to know truth with absolute certainty. The best we can hope for is relative or reasonable certainty.

During the course of researching and writing, I tried to remain faithful to these principles. I must admit that sometimes the evidence was very convincing and easy to believe; but it is also true that some evidence seemed less credible and remains questionable. However, on the whole, I come away from this project with a strong conviction that the theory that Jesus had planned the shocking climax to his Palestinian Ministry, was rescued, healed and embarked on an Asian Ministry, is very credible. Am I positive? Of course not! But I have what Professor Bertocci used to call reasonable and I would add existential certainty. Using the comprehensive coherence test of truth, I am convinced that the "survival theory" about Jesus fits with more data and provides better explanations than the conventional "death on the Cross" theory.

The second challenge for me was theological, and it was the greater. Seminary trained at Boston University and an ordained Minister in the United Methodist Church, I had subscribed, without question, to the powerful doctrine that "Christ died for our sins." How could I surrender that belief, the core belief, so it seemed, and remain a faithful Christian? And yet, my continuing study of religion led me to the Qur'an, the Gnostic Gospels, and a constant production of scholarly material that suggested alternative ideas that resulted in this project. As noted above, this exercise brought me to intellectually accept the "survival theory." But, what is much more important to my practicing Christian faith was the dawning realization that my faith had not crumbled, but, in fact, had grown stronger. It was as if my faith had been released from a dogma—always very difficult to understand and explain to others—and was now free to soar into unlimited realms of spiritual speculation and revelation.

No longer need I believe that somehow a loving parent-like God planned to make a blood sacrifice of his Son or that such an offering could have ethical import.

No longer need I believe that a supernatural miracle of Resurrection was necessary to prove God's love, seal Jesus' Ministry, and ensure us of our immortality.

Now, I can at least ponder alternative theories about an Asian ministry of post-crucifixion Jesus found in the Qur'an and the ongoing discovery of scrolls that reveal fascinating stories about Jesus, heretofore unknown.

Now, I can engage in the continuing and rewarding reevaluation of the many dimensions of meaning about the life and teachings of Jesus.

Now what is the bottom line for me—and for Christians? First of all, my faith remains intact. I still proclaim that for me, Jesus is the "pioneer and perfector of my faith" (Heb. 12:1, 2). I mean his insightful teachings distilled from the Jewish torah, and most of all, his unparallel revelation of the divine nature, remain as striking for me today as they were for the first disciples. To be brought into Jesus' presence is to come into God's presence. Jesus was the God-filled person. Tillich once said: "Jesus made his life transparent, so we could see God." Jesus is truly the Christ of faith. Moreover, as we have shown in our analysis of the Fourth Gospel, that affirmation is not only grounded in the confession of devout believers but is reinforced by what we believe we have shown to be the literal statements of the mature Jesus. I believe that we can now confidentially affirm that the Jesus of history and the Christ of faith are two aspects of one person.

Theologians have tended to separate the two with "Jesus of history" referring to the earthly life of the human Jesus of Nazareth and "Christ of Faith" referring to the divine Son of God who for a time lived on Earth in human form and after His ascension is available to every believer as the eternal Holy Spirit. Shehan in his book *The First Coming* distinguishes between the "pre-Easter" and "post-Easter" Jesus.[1] However, I have reached a different understanding sparked by my Upanishadic hermeneutic reading of the Fourth Gospel. After completing his first Palestinian Ministry, Jesus left Palestine as the Jesus of history. After a decade of study and missionary work in Asia, he returned to his homeland as the Christ of faith. We have carefully explained that we do not believe that this means that Jesus had somehow transmuted into deity. Rather, we believe that Jesus had gained a clarified understanding of who he was, and who we all can become. Let us use the word deity to mean literally God and the word divine to mean God-like. With this understanding, we may say that Jesus could announce his divinity, certainly not his deity, as exemplified by the dramatic "I am" sayings. On this interpretation, "Christ" will mean not literally God but the one who reveals God most clearly.

We could conclude by saying that we have discovered the missing link between the Jesus of history and the Christ of faith. I remember years ago hearing liberal theologian Kirby Page challenges us with the words: "You must choose Jesus or Christ!" There is some truth in those words if we are bound by conventional theology; but using our interpretation, we can move beyond that challenge for we know it to be a false dichotomy. The mature Jesus, the missing link, has shown us what has always been true. Jesus of history and Christ of faith are grounded in one very remarkable person who showed us that what we call human and divine are two aspects of each one of us. It is, of course, clear to me that this kind of faith would not be acceptable to many, probably most, Christians. They still accept the paradigm that Jesus was the human disguised deity that descended from heaven, performed an act of salvation, and rose from Earth to return to his heavenly home in the Trinity. I must say, as gently as possible, out of respect for the millions, living and dead, of faithful Christians, that this is a paradigm that must be broken!

This brings us to the second effect of this seismic theological moment. I earnestly believe that as more and more Christians escape dogmatic theology through education and spiritual experience, they will belatedly recognize the spiritual kinship that has always existed between all theists: Christians, Jews, and Moslems, and let us include Hindu Brahmanists, Buddhists, and Taoists, because there are other features besides theism that all religions share. Jesus opened the doors between several religions in India, Tibet, and China, thereby allowing the spiritual winds to freely circulate between the great religious traditions and produce very practical results. Consider these examples.

Brahmanism, especially in the form of Vedanta, can enrich our appreciation and understanding of the cosmic dimensions of each individual soul as a poise of being for God on Earth. Gandhi used this insight to promote *satyagraha*, his very practical non-violent program of liberation theology that Martin Luther King further developed and successfully employed in the cause of Black liberation in America. Both of these great men acknowledged the combined impact of Jesus and Vedanta on their lives.

Taosim carries within it the seeds of an ecological ethics that we so very desperately need if life on our planet Earth is to survive. The *Jesus Sutras* showed us that Taoist sensitivity realizes that nature and humanity fit perfectly with Jesus' reverence for nature and non-violent ethos. Jesus' Way and the Way of the Tao are congruent in their emphasis on the respect that ought to be accorded all persons. No slavery of any kind and no violence can be tolerated!

Perhaps the greatest impact that Jesus made upon Eastern religions is to be found in Mahayana Buddhism. We have tried to make a reasonable case for our conclusion that Jesus arrived in India at a very propitious time during the evolution of Buddhism from a very effective psychology of self-control to a true religion grounded in the experience of the Cosmic Buddha Mind that inhabits all beings. We believe it was Jesus who made the strongest case for theism by witnessing to his own profound experience of his heavenly Father-God. Moreover, Jesus' dramatic insistence that we should love all of God's children fits perfectly with the Buddhist demand for compassion for all persons and creatures throughout the universe.

Islam has interacted with Jesus in quite a different way. Of course, Jesus could not impact Islam in a personal way as we have suggested he did with the other faiths. The religion founded by Muhammad did not exist and would not come into formal existence for another six hundred years. However, upon reading the Qur'an, one will discover that the Qur'an refers to Jesus in terms of great respect for his gospel of ethical love and his exemplary life of piety and devotion to his heavenly Father-God. I suggest that as the interfaith dialogue develops, Muslims will discover increasingly how Jesus' non-violent ethos very closely corresponds with Muhammad's own spirit of ethical love that included teaching his followers to avoid violence and reach out to all other theists. Of course, Jesus knew only of Jewish theists. But, I am sure that had he a fuller understanding of the other religions, he would have included them as well. Moreover, from the perspective of this present study, we must remember that it was from the Qur'an that we discovered the tradition about Jesus' escape from death on the cross. In this sense, we owe a very great deal to Islam, for without that initial impetus, our theory would probably not have been developed.

As dramatic as these examples are, they identify only the first stage of what I believe will be a swelling evolutionary movement toward a new world culture. It will be characterized in the religious dimensions by a new and higher level of spirituality that will draw upon the insights of all of the great world religions. This is not a call for a grand mixing of all religions. I accept as a truism, that there are many pathways to God and spirituality that culminate in communion with God, however expressed.[2] Each path has it's own charm and coherence with the culture that helped shape it. But even as we follow different paths, we are now at least learning to communicate across cultures with our brothers and sisters who have important values to share with us.

Missionary sharing can be a good thing, for each of the several traditions, as long as it is free from arrogant dogmatism and is open to listening to the devotes from other faiths. The new ecumenical movement must reach beyond the dogmatic certainty that "my religion is the only true faith" and enter into dialogue with *all* the other faiths. This powerful, new dialectic must be a two-way street of witnessing and "deep listening," to use the phrase of Thich Nhat Hanh. Hopefully, this way of mutual respect will help guide us ever closer to God's new world order envisioned by the Hebrew prophets, Jesus, and many seers from the other religions. I believe that it was Jesus' second, heretofore, secret ministry that can guide us to the realization of Isaiah's great vision:

> In days to come
>   the mountain of the LORD's house
> shall be established as the
>   highest of the mountains, . . .
> Many peoples shall come and
>   say
> "Come, let us go up to the
>   mountain of the LORD, . . .
> He shall judge between the nations,
>   and shall arbitrate for many peoples;

they shall beat their swords into plowshares,
and their spears into pruning hooks;
nation shall not life up sword against nation,
neither shall they learn war any more."

(Isaiah 2:2-4)

Glossary

Abba: Jesus' name for God: Father
Aham asmi: I am
Aham Brahm asmi: Hindu term: I am Brahman
Aham chita: I am mind or light
Aham jiva: I am life
Aham sattya: I am truth
Aham yoga: I am the way
Ahriman: The God of Evil in Persian Zoroastrian religion
Ahura Mazada: The God of Truth and Good in Persian Zoroastrian religion
Anatman: Buddhist term meaning no immortal soul
Anicca: Buddhist term meaning process or impermance
Arjuna: Leading Hindu knight in the Maghabhrata (great war)
Ashoka: Indian King who sent Buddhist missionaries to the West
Atman: Hindu term for soul (human and divine)
Avatar: Personal incarnation of a Hindu God
Beatitude: part of Jesus' Sermon on the Mount listing the key virtues
Bhagavad Gita: portion of the Mahabhratta Epic featuring Lord Krishna's sermon to Arjuna
Bodhisattva: Buddhist Saint or one who aspire to be a Buddha
Brahma: Hindu God of Creation (personal)
Brahman: Hindu term for the Ground of all Being (beyond the personal)
Brahmin: Hindu priestly cast
Buddha: The Enlightened teacher, founder of Buddhism (see also Sidhartha Gautama).
Christ Cult: belief that Jesus was the divine Lord who came to offer salvation by offering Himself as a blood sacrifice to pay for our sins
Christ of faith: term referring to Jesus as resurrected Savior
Christ: Greek term for Messiah originally. Later, Savior Lord
Christology: theological term referring to the life and saving work of Jesus
Codependent Origination: There is no "First Cause" Creator. Everything emerges out of a confluence of entities and forces.
Davidic Messiah: belief the Messiah would be a military hero (liberator) and political (King) leader of the Jews
Deutero Isaiah: poet prophet of the Babylonian Exile (also II Isaiah)
Devil: Source of Evil and Ruler of demons in Hell (also Satan)
Dharmakaya: Cosmic Buddha Mind in Buddhist Trinity
Eight-fold Path: steps for attaining Buddhist Enlightenment: Right understanding, aspiration, speech, actions, vocation, effort, mindfulness, and meditation
Essenes: Jewish Sect in Qumran Community; taught healing and non-violence
Faith Healing: healing cannot occur if patient lacks belief (faith) that God's power is working through the healer (also psychosomatic healing)
Five Attributes: Buddhist term for the components of a person (see Skandas)– body, mind, perceptions., karma, and will

Fourth Noble Truths: Buddhas' teaching of the cause and cure of suffering. Suffering is universal, caused by craving, can be cured by extinguishing the selfish ego. (see Eight-fold Path)

Gnostic Gospels: non-canonical Gospels of Gnostic Christians presenting Jesus as a teacher of a mystical path to salvation emphasizing meditation and metaphysical knowledge

Hadith: the extra Qur'anic Sayings of Muhammad

Hermeneutic: critical interpretation of a text

Honored One: Chinese name for God in the Jesus Sutras

"I am" sayings: used by Jesus in the Fourth Gospel. (See also the "Aham" sayings in the Bhagavad Gita)

Issa: Indian name for Jesus

Jainism: An Indian religion stressing non-violence and reverence for all living beings.

Jesus of history: Denotes the life and teachings of Jesus of Nazareth contra the theological "Christ of Faith"

Jesus people: Original followers of Jesus who were impressed by his charismatic person, inspiring teachings about God's plan to establish a new world community of justice and peace and his power to heal and inspire faith in God. They regarded him as Rabbi and Prophet.

Jesus Sutras: ancient Chinese scrolls and stone slates containing stories about Jesus teaching to Buddhists and Taoists

Judas: disciple and friend of Jesus who may have played a positive rule in Jesus' Crucifixion/Resurrection Drama.

Karma: Hindu belief in a cosmic ethical law that provides appropriate responses to every act even controlling the reincarnation process according to what one has earned in terms of ethical living.

Karuna: Buddhist term for compassion and the highest virtue

Koinonia: Greek term for "beloved community" used to denote the Kingdom of God

Krishna: Avator (incarnation) of Vishu, Lord of the Moral Law and persona in the Trimurti (Hindu Trinity)

Kshatriyas: The Warrior Clans in the Hindu Caste system

Last Supper: Jesus' last meal with his disciples in which he prepares for the Crucifixion.

Logos: Greek term for "word." In Stoic philosophy "Creative Wisdom." And in Christian theology the divine Wisdom God uses to Crate the world.

Mahayana Buddhism: The theistic expression of Buddhism that regards Buddha as the incarnation of the Cosmic Dharmakaya Buddha Mind.

Mary Magdalene: Discipline of Jesus, called his Companion and may have been his wife. Regarded by many as his "beloved disciple."

Maya: The natural world is an illusion–a dream of Brahma

Messiah: In Hebrew Bible, any one called by God and anointed to perform an important task for Israel.

messianic banquet: The traditional Jewish belief that when the final Messiah comes, he will offer free food and drink to everyone–especially the poor and outcast.

Muhammad: The founder of Islam whose teachings are found in the Qur'an.

Muslim: A follower of Islam who worships Allah (Arabic name for God) and honors Muhammad as the Prophet of God.

Mystery religions: worship of Savior Gods often including sacred meals of their flesh and blood believed to impart saving grace

Nirmanakaya (Gautama Sidhartha Buddha): The human manifestation of the Cosmic Buddha in the Buddhist Trinity

"Only Way" formula: denotes the most valuable spiritual teaching of a prophet or founder

Original Nature: Taoist term expressing the essential goodness of human persons

Palestian Gospels: accounts of Jesus' life and teaching during his residence in Palestine

Pali: language of Buddhist literature as contrasted with Hindu Sanskrit

pan-en-theism: theological terms that represents a synthesis of theism (God is completely transcendent) and pantheism (God is completely immanent). God is intimately related to every part of nature, but more than nature in every respect.

pantheism: the belief that all of Nature is God

Patya Samutpada (Pali) Paticca Samuppada (Sanskrit): Buddhish doctrine of multiple causation

personalism: The philosophy that personhood is the highest value that we know. Not limited to finite human persons.

prophetic drama: refers to the theatrical technique employed by the Hebrew prophets and Jesus

pudgala: Buddhist term for personal soul

Qur'an: the teachings of Mohammad regarded as sacred and reveled by the angel Gabriel

Rabbi Yeshua: title given to Jesus by Jews while he resided in Palestine

realized eschatology: belief that the End Time is being progressively manifested in history (immanent in history)

Shiva: Lord of the cosmic samsara process in the Hindu Trinity.

Skandas: The five parts of the human being: mind, body, perceptions, karma, and will

Suffering Servant: Deutaro Isaiah's portrayal of Israel in Babylonian Captivity who inspires vicarious suffering to the world for the purpose of teaching the consequence of not living according to God's Moral Law

Syriac Christian texts: Contain traditions of Jesus and Thomas in India

Tao te King (or Ching): philosophical book of Taoism attributed to Lao Tzu the founder

Taoism: mystical nature religion about Tao as Ground of all Being manifested as Yang (active forces) and Yin (passive quality) (Taoist Trinity)

Tat tuam assi: Hindu expression–and you are also divine

Tathagata: a name for the Buddha. One who is not there.

Theraveda Buddhism: Earliest School–non-theistic, atomistic cosmology, and psychology

Tibetan Buddhism: teaches that enlightenment can be attained instantaneously in this life. Contains exotic symbolism from the earlier Bon reigion

Torah: Gods Law also the first five books in the Hebrew Bible

Transmigration: also reincarnation The Hindu and Buddhist doctrine of rebirth based on the karma merit earned in previous life (lives)

Trikaya: Buddhist Trinity: Dharmakaya (Cosmic Buddha Mind), Sambogakaya (Heavenly Buddha Spirit), Nirmanakaya (human manifestation of Buddha, Gautama Sidhartha)

Trimurti: The Hindu Trinity: Brahma, Shiva, and Vishnu. Gods of Creation, Samsara, and Morality

Trinity, Christian: Doctrine of God as three Persons–Father, Creator, Son, incarnate Savior, and guiding Holy Spirit

Upanishads: the philosophical portion of the Vedas

Vedas: Original Hindu Scriptures in four parts, culminating in the Upanishads

Virgin birth (or virgin conception): Doctrine of the Christ cult that Jesus was conceived by Holy Spirit and born by the Virgin Mary

Vishnu: Member of the Hindu Trinity (Trimurti), Savior Lord who manifests himself periodically when humans need guidance

wu wei: Golden Rule of Taoism: Live naturally, never do more than is necessary to live in harmony with Nature

Yahweh: Early Hebrew name of God. "I AM. . . ."

Ye Su: Name given to Jesus in China

Yoga: Hindu disciplines for body, mind, and spirit–Hatha, Karma, Jnana

Bibliography

The Bhagavad-Gita: Krishna's Counsel in Time of War. Trans by Barbara Sfolor Miller, Bantam Books, N.Y., 1986.

The Bible, New Revised Standard Versions, Collins, N.Y., 1996.

The Jewish Study Bible, Tanakh Translation, Jewish Publication Society, N.Y., 2004,.

The Complete Gospels: Annotated Scholars Version. Revised and Expanded Edition, Robert J. Miller, Ed. A Polubridge Press Book, 1992. Harper Collens, San Francisco, 1994.

The Holy Qur'an. Trans and Commentary by Maulana Muhammad Ali, pub. Ahmadyyah Anjuman Isha, at Islam Press, Lahore, Inc., USA, Columbus, OH, 1995.

The Random House Dictionary of the English Language, 2nd Ed., Unabridged, Random House, N.Y., 1987.

Abernathy, George L. and Langford, Thomas A. *Philosophy of Religion,* 2nd Ed. Macmillan Co., N.Y., 1968.

Angus, Samuel, *The Mystery-Religions and Christianity.* Carol Publishing Group, NY, 1966. Originally by Charles Scribner's Sons 1925.

Baigent, Michael, Leigh, Richard, and Lincoln, Henry, *Holy Blood, Holy Grail.* Bantam Doubleday, Dell Publishing Group, Inc., NY:, 1983.

Baillie, D. M., *God Was In Christ,* Scribner's, N.Y., 1948.

Bejamin, Joshua M. *The Mystery of Israel's Ten Lost Tribes and The Legend of Jesus in India.* Mosaic Books, New Delhi, 2001.

Bertocci, Peter A. *An Introduction to the Philosophy of Religion,* Prentice Hall, N.J., 1951.

Brightman, Edger S. *A Philosophy of Religion.* Prentice Hall, N.J., 1950.

Burkitt, F. C. *Early Christianity Outside the Roman Empire.* Cambridge University Press, 1899, Gorgias Press (Reprint Series), 2002.

Carus, Paul, *The Gospel of Buddha.* Open Court, LaSalle, IL, 1990.

Chilton, Bruce, *Rabbi Jesus.* Doubleday, Random House, NY, 2002.

Crossan, John Dominic. *The Essential Jesus,* Harper Collins, NY, 1994.

———, *Jesus, A Revolutionary Biography,* Harper Collins, N.Y., 1995.

DeWolf, L. Harold. *Theology of the Living Church,* Harper & Row, N.Y., 1968.

Feng, Gai-Fu, and English, Jane. *The Tao Te Ching.* Random House, NY, 1972.

Funk, Robert W. and The Jesus Seminar, *The Complete Gospels,* Macmillan, N.Y., 1993.

———, *Honest to Jesus,* Harper Collins, NY, 1997.

Fung, Yu Lan, *A Short History of Chinese Philosophy,* Macmillan, N.Y., 1960.

Gardinar, Laurence. *Bloodline of Holy Blood, Holy Grail.* Barnes and Noble Books, NY, 1996.

Goodspeed, Edgar J. *Strange New Gospels,* Books for Libraries Press. First Published 1931, Reprinted 1971.

Hanh, Thich Nhat, *Coming Home: Jesus and Buddha As Brothers.* Penguin Putnam, Inc., NY, 1999.

Hordern, Walter. *A Layman's Guide to Protestant Theology.* Revised Edition. MacMillan, NY, 1986.

Jansma, T. *A Selection From the Acts of Judas Thomas,* Leiden, E. J. Brill, 1982.

Khalidi, Tarif, *The Muslim Jesus: Sayings and Stories in Islamic Literature,* Harvard University Press, Cambridge, Mass: 2001.

Knudson, Albert. *The Doctrine of Redemption,* Abingdon-Cokesburg, 1933.

Koller, John, *Oriental Philosophies,* 1st ed. Charles Scribner's Sons, NY, 1970.

Larson, Martin. *The Religion of the Occident*. Littlefield & Adams, NJ, 1961.

Mack, Burton, L., *The Lost Gospel: The Book of Q*. Harper, San Francisco, CA, 1993.

Moraes, Frank, and Howe, Edward, Eds. *India*. McGraw-Hill, NY: 1974.

Mountcastle, Wm. W. *Religion in Planetary Perspective*, Abingdon Cokesbury Press, Nashville, TN, 1979.

———, *Science Fantasy Voices and Visions of Cosmic Religion*. University Press of America, MD, 1995.

Palmer, Martin. *The Jesus Sutras*, Ballantine Wellspring, The Ballantine Publish Group, NY, 2001.

Pfeiffer, Robert. *Introduction to the Old Testament*. Harper & Brothers, NY, 1941.

Prabhavananda, Swami and Manchester, Frederick. *The Upanishads*. The New American Library of World Literature, Vedanta Press, Hollywood, CA, 1964.

Price, Shelby. *Interpreting the New Testament*, Holt, N.Y., 1961.

Prophet, Elizabeth Clare. *The Lost Years of Jesus*. Summit University Press, Livingston, MT, 1984.

Renan, Earnest. *The Life of Jesus*. Prometheus Books, Great Mind Series, NY, 1991.

Robinson, James. *The Nag Hammadi Library*, Harper Collins, N.Y., 1990.

Schonfield, Hugh J. *The Passover Plot*. Element Books, Ltd., Worcester, England, 1985.

Shehan, Thomas. *The First Coming*. Random House, NY, 1986.

Smith, Morton. *The Secret Gospel*. Harper & Row, NY, 1973.

Spong, John Shelby. *Born of a Woman*. Harper San Francisco, (Harper Collins 1992).

Taylor, Vincent. "The Life and Ministry of Jesus." *The Interpreter's Bible, Vol. VII*. Abingdon Cokesburg Press, Nashville, N.Y., 1951.

Zimmer, Heinrich, *Philosophies of India*, Ed. Joseph Campbell Meridian Books. The World Publishing Co. Cleveland & N.Y., 1961.

Index

Endnotes

Chapter One
1. *The Qur'an* Ch. 4, The Women, Part VI, v.157.
2. *Holy Blood, Holy Grail*, pp. 352-358.
3. *The Passover Plot*, pp. 162-181.

Chapter Two
1. *Introduction to the Old Testament*, p. 570.

Chapter Three
1. *Rabbi Jesus*, pp. 217, 253. See also *Jesus: A Revolutionary Biography*, pp. 59, 70 by J. Dominic Crossan.
2. *The Interpreter's Bible, Vol. VII*, "The Life Ministry of Jesus," pp. 137-138.
3. *Interpreting the New Testament*, p. 240-245 (1st ed.) See also *Jesus, A Revolutionary Biography*, pp. 46-48, by John Dominic Crossan.
4. *A Theology of the Living Church*, pp. 311-316.
5. *Holy Blood, Holy Grail*, pp. 338-339.
6. *Ibid.*, pp. 318 ff and *The Complete Gospels*, The Jesus Seminar, p. 408.
7. *The Secret Gospel*, pp. 14-17, 38.
8. *Ibid.*, 47-52.
9. *Holy Blood, Holy Grail*, pp. 321, 373.
10. *The Lost Gospel*, pp. 215-223. Burton Mack notes: "It was in the Christ cult, not in the Jesus movement, that the Christian notion of conversion as a personal transformation emerged." (p. 220) "The difference between the Jesus movement and their mythologies and the congregations of the Christ and their mythologies should now be clear. One important contrast is that between a focus on the instructions of a teacher and the dramatic event of a martyr's death and resurrection." (p. 221).
11. *Ezra*, Ch. 9, 10; *Nehemiah*, 13:27-30.
12. *The Jewish Study Bible*, Tanakh Translation Is 53: 8, 9. Scholars debate whether these lines describe the literal death of the servant or the severe straits he was in. Exaggerated descriptions of one's plight as equivalent to death are common in the Bible (p. 892).
13. *The Passover Plot*, p. 162. "Provided that crucifixion was not too prolonged, it was possible for the life of the victim to be saved. First hand information about this is furnished by Josephus. He tells us in his autobiography that during the last siege of Jerusalem by the Romans . . . he passed a number of prisoners who had been crucified, and recognized three of them as acquaintances. . . . He went to Titus and pleaded for them. Titus ordered that they should be taken down and given the best possible treatment. Two of them died but the third recovered. The indications are that these men had been on the cross longer than was Jesus, yet even so one of them survived."
14. *A Layman's Guide to Protestant Theology*, pp. 25-28, *Doctrine of Redemption*, pp. 357-369. See also *God Was in Christ*, D. M. Baillie, pp. 190-202.
15. "Mythology in the New Testament," Rudolph Bultmann., pp. 347-349, in *Philosophy of Religion*, 2nd Ed., Abernathy and Langford.
16. *Rabbi Jesus*, pp. 186, 187, 227, 228.
17. Could this Judas be the same Judas identified as Jesus' brother who also had the name Thomas? See Chapter 4. f.n. 14 regarding the two names.
18. *Passover Plot*, pp. 135, 136.
19. *The Nag Hammadi Library*, pp. 365-366.

20. *The Qur'an*, commentary, p. 237, 238.

21. *The Passover Plot*, pp. 162-181.

22. *Blood Line of the Holy Grail*, pp. 352-357.

23. *Jesus in India*, p. 55.

24. *Ibid.*, pp. 56, 57.

25. *Ibid.*, p. 57.

26. *Ibid.*, pp. 55, f.n. 3.

27. *Strange New Gospels*, pp. 31-41.

28. *The Lost Gospel*, pp. 215-223.

29. *The Nag Hammodi Library*, pp. 525, 526.

30. *Born of a Woman*, pp. 187-199, Spong argues that the marriage at Cana (in John's gospel) is really the marriage of Jesus and Mary Magdalene.

31. *The Life of Jesus*, Earnest Renan, p. 215. "For the historian, the life of Jesus finishes with his last sigh. But such was the impression he had left in the heart of his disciples and of a few devoted women that during some weeks more it was as if he were living and consoling them. Had his body been taken away, or did enthusiasm, always credulous, create afterwards the group of narratives by which it was sought to establish faith in the resurrection?"

32. *Ibid.*, pp. 60, 61.

33. *Philosophies of India*, pp. 496-497, "King Ashoka is said to have supported sixty four thousand Buddhist monks. . . . Missionaries were sent forth. . . Ashoka sent teachers of the Buddhist Dharma to Antiochus II of Syria, Ptolemy II of Egypt, Magas of Cyrene, Antigonus Gonatas of Macedonia, and Alexander II of Epirus." (Recorded in Askoka's Rock Edict XIII, Cf Vincent A. Smith, *The Edicts of Askoka*, London, 1909, p. 20).

Chapter Four

1. Professor Lal Goel reminds me that Kashmir is historically a part of Greater India and not a separate nation. I have followed my source in making the distinction between India and Kashmir.

2. *The Religion of the Occident*, pp. 284-292.

3. *Legend of Jesus*, p. 62.

4. *Early Christianity*, p. 4.

5. *Ibid.*, pp. 5, 7.

6. *Ibid.*, 8, 9, 13, 14.

7. *Ibid.*, pp. 76-78.

8. *Ibid.*, p. 83, 84.

9. Burkitt includes a copy of *Acts* in Syriac, but I have used Benjamin's English translation in *Jesus in India*, p. 62.

10. *http://www.piney.com/Apoc_Acts_of_Thomas.html*. This is from the internet source for the complete English translation.

11. *Legend of Jesus*, p. 63. For those who would protest that the Bethlehem tradition is late, Bruce Chilton argues that there is a north Bethlehem not far from Nazareth (*Rabbi Jesus*, p. 8-9).

12. *Ibid.*, p. 64.

13. *Matthew* 13:55-56 and *Mark* 6:3.

14. *The Gospel of Thomas, Annotated Scholars Version*, p. 305. Robert funk notes that the Fellows of Jesus Seminar offer a fresh translation of this gospel discovered among the Nag Hammad's texts in Egypt in 1945. The commentary on the passage quoted above notes that the name(s) Didymos Judas Thomas appears elsewhere only in the *Syrian Acts of Thomas* but Judas Thomas occurs in several Syrian manuscripts of

John 14:22. Furthermore, only Judas is a bona fide name. Didymos and Thomas are Greek and Syrian words for twin. However, Thomas is used as a given name in other passages. The commentary adds "Thomas was thought by the early church to have evangelized eastern Syria and India . . . (*but this*) is a matter for further investigation." I submit that the data included in our investigation constitutes a strong argument that Judas Thomas carried the Gospel of India in the company of his twin brother Jesus. Note that the words of the Prologue refer to a *living* Jesus whose sayings were recorded by didymos Thomas. I am convinced that twin brother Thomas was speaking of his very much alive brother Jesus. Moreover, I believe that this gospel contained the sayings that Jesus brought back from his Asian ministry when he returned to Palestine. The Fellows find Gnosticism in this gospel because it speaks of this evil world and calls us to discover our true identity as children of God. But we will provide data in a following chapter that supports an Indian origin, specifically in the Upanishads.

15. Internet Source, p. 1.

16. *Ibid.*, p. 4.

17. *Ibid.*, pp. 4-5.

18. *Legend of Jesus*, pp. 84, 85.

19. *The Random House Dictionary of the English Language*. 2nd Ed., Unabridged. Random House, NY. 1987.

Chapter Five

1. *The Lost Years of Jesus*, p. 18, 19.

2. *Strange New Gospels*, pp. 15, 16., f.n.2

3. *Ibid.*, p. 117, f.n. 3.

4. *Lost Years of Jesus.*, p. 46 ff.

5. *Ibid.*, p. 50, 51.

6. *Ibid.*, p. 54.

7. *Ibid.*, p. 55.

8. *The Lost Years of Jesus*, p. 30 ff. and *Strange New Gospels*, pp. 22, 23.

9. *The Lost Years of Jesus*, p. 37 ff.

10. The Priests who taught Issa to read the Vedas in Sanskrit must also have taught him some of the vernacular languages to enable him to teach the common people or perhaps, more likely, he spoke through a merchant interpreter who knew Jesus' Aramaic language.

11. *Oriental Philosophies*, p. 131-139.

12. *Ibid.*, p. 152-153.

13. *A Philosophy of Religion*, p. 230

14. *Romans* 1:19, 20.

15. *The Lost Years of Jesus*, p. 225.

16. *Ibid*, pp. 44, 45.

17. *Ibid.*, p. 237.

18. *Ibid.*, f.n., p. 236.

19. *Altain Himalaya*, pp. 257, 258, and *Himalya*, pp. 130-132.

20. *Ibid.*, p. 261 and *Heart of Asia*, pp. 29, 30, quoted in the *Lost Years of Jesus*.

21. *Ibid.*, p. 263 from his diary "Letters from America" the eighth of September 1925.

22. *Ibid.*, p. 265.

23. *Ibid.*, p. 270.

24. *Isaiah*, 49:1-6.

Chapter Six
1. *The Jesus Sutras*, p. 42. Palmer and his team of translators have added the chapters and verses.
2. *Ibid.*, p. 45.
3. *Ibid.*, p. 62.
4. *Ibid.*, p. 63.
5. *Oriental Philosophies*, pp. 140-141. These Buddhists were called Pudgalavadins.
6. *Op Cit.*, pp. 64, 68.
7. *Ibid.*, p. 68.
8. *Ibid.*, p. 140.
9. *Ibid.*, p. 141.
10. *Ibid.*, p. 143.
11. *Religion in Planetary Perspective*, pp. 159-161.
12. *The Jesus Sutres.*, p. 147.
13. *Ibid.*
14. *Religion in Planetary Perspective*, pp. 116-117.
15. Regarding Jesus' name in China; Ye Su could be a transliteration of Jesus or it could be the Chinese word for "justice," Yi or Ye, followed by Su or Tzu that means "sage." Hence, The Just Sage or Master. I prefer the latter reconstruction.
16. *Op. Cit.*, p. 175.
17. *Op. Cit.*, p. 190.
18. *Ibid.*, pp. 198-200.
19. *Ibid.* p. 201.

Chapter Seven
1. Matthew 17:20 and Luke 17:5, 6.
2. *The Gospel of Buddha*, pp. 209-212, Buddhaghosha's Parables, Trans T. Rogers, London, 1870, pp. 98 ff.
3. *John* 4:7-15.
4. *The Gospel of Buddha*, pp. 196-197. Burnouf, *Introduction, à l'histoire du Bouddhisme Indian*, Paris, 1844.
5. *Mark* 6:45-52; *Matthew* 14:22-33.
6. *The Gospel of Buddha*, pp. 212, 213, Chinese Dhammapada. Trans. S. Beal, London and Boston, 1878.
7. *John* 9:1-41.
8. *The Gospel of Buddha*, p. 181, The Dhammapada, Trans., F. Max Müller, Vol. X, Part I, *Sacred Books of the East*, Oxford, 1881.
9. *Matthew* 13:47
10. *Tao te Ching*, Ch. 73.
11. *Matthew* 6:25-30.
12. *Tao te Ching*, Ch. 51.
13. *Ibid.*, Ch. 37.
14. *Ibid.*, Ch. 41.
15. *Ibid.*, Ch. 48.
16. *Matthew* 11:25, 26.
17. *Matthew* 18: 1-14.
18. *Matthew* 23:11, 12.
19. *Mark* 10:17, 18; *Matthew* 19:17; *Luke* 18:19.
20. *Tao te Ching*, Ch. 10.
21. *Ibid.*, Ch. 28.

22. *Ibid.*, Ch. 49.
23. *Ibid.*, Ch. 13.
24. *Matthew* 26:51, 52. John alone identifies Peter as the defender (John 18:10).
25. *Tao te Ching*, Ch. 30.
26. *Ibid.*, Ch. 31.
27. *Ibid.*, Ch. 42.
28. *Ibid.*, Ch. 61.
29. *John* 1:1-9.
30. *The Aitareya Upanishad*, *The Upanishads* Tran. Swami Prebhavananda and Frederick Manchester.
31. The spelling Brahman refers to Ultimate Reality beyond personal attributes. Brahma, without the final "n" refers to the One as God the Person.
32. *John* 14:11.
33. *John* 17:20-22.
34. See Bultmann's *Gospel of John*, p. 679.
35. See Bishop Spongs' *Born Of A Woman*, Ch. 8, for a very thoughtful analysis of the "Wedding at Cana."
36. Perhaps we should say, one of the earliest gospels, noting that Proto-Mark may have also been composed during this same early period. Clearly, Matthew and Luke are later Gospels, that reflect the developing Christian theology, complete with virgin birth and resurrection appearances that are absent from the earliest versions of Mark and "John" (sic.) Mary.
37. *The Muslim Jesus*, pp. 6, 7.
38. *Ibid.*, pp. 122, 123.
39. *Ibid.*, p. 141.
40. *Ibid.*, 164.
41. *Ibid.*, p. 2.
42. *Ibid.*, p. 15.
43. *The Essential Jesus*, John Dominic Crossan.
44. *John* 21:25.

Chapter Eight
1. *The Lost Gospel*, See Chapter 11, "Mythmaking and the Christ," pp. 207-225.
Honest to Jesus, p. 312, See #17, "We will have to abandon the doctrine of the blood atonement."
The Mystery Religions and Christianity. See Foreword and Chapter II "What Is A Mystery Religion", p. 39 ff.
2. *The Mythmaker: Paul, the Man Who Invented Christianity.*
3. *Oriental Philosophies*, p. 129.
4. *Ibid.*, pp. 119-123.
5. *Jesus and Buddha As Brothers*, pp. 195-200.
6. *Science Fantasy Voices and Visions of Cosmic Religion*, pp. 130, 131.
7. *Bloodline of Holy Blood, Holy Grail*, p. 82, from Andreas Faber-Kaiser *Jesus Died in Kashmir*, Abacus, Sphere, London, 1978.
8. *Jesus in India*, p. 95.
9. *Ibid.*
10. *Bloodline of Holy Blood, Holy Grail*, p. 358, see f.n. 30, Notes and References, p. 473. I must admit that this claim does not have strong scholarly support. The name of the Australian journalist called Joyce is vague, and I have not seen a copy of the alleged *Jesus Scroll*.

11. *Science Fantasy Voices and Visions of Cosmic Religion*, pp. 68, 73.

12. *Hebrew* 12:1-2a ". . . let us run with perseverance the race that is set before us looking to Jesus the pioneer and perfector of our faith."

Chapter Nine

1. *The First Coming*, p. 131 ff.

2. Religion in Planetary Perspective, pp. 8, 176. Sci Fantasy Voices – Visions of Cosmic Religions, pp. 56.

About the Author

The author earned his Ph.D. in Systematic Theology from Boston University where he was Teaching Assistant for Dr. L. Harold DeWolf and took courses from Dr. Paul Tillich at Harvard. He is an ordained Minister in the United Methodist Church. He has taught at High Point College, Nebraska Wesleyan University where he was Chair of the Department of Philosophy, Florida Southern College, and the University of West Florida where he is presently Emeritus Marvie L. Tipton Professor of Philosophy and Religious Studies.

In addition to articles published in academic journals, he has authored *Religion in Planetary Perspective: A Philosophy of Comparative Religion* (Abingdon Press) and *Science Fantasy Voices and Visions of Cosmic Religion* (University Press of America).